# ACADIAN ACADEMICS

# Five Practice Tests
## for the
# Upper Level ISEE®

D1724467

Chad Mills
Acadian Academics
Manhattan, NY

® ISEE is a registered trademark of the Educational Records Bureau, which was not involved in the production of, and does not endorse, this book.

Five Practice Tests for the Upper Level ISEE, First Edition
Acadian Academics
New York, NY
Copyright © 2014 Jarrad Mills
ISBN-13: 978-1-495329-07-4

Note: *Independent School Entrance Exam* is a registered trademark of Educational Records Bureau, which does not endorse this product.

# Contents

# Acknowledgments

I am deeply indebted to a number of people without whose contributions this book would not have been possible: to Emily Vanston, who supplied three of the reading comprehension passages; to Jordanna Brodsky, Jason Mills, and Ben Mills, all of whom assisted with the editing process; to Lindsey Wells, who lent her visual eye to the cover art; to my students, whose feedback was essential in drafting clear and appropriate questions; and lastly, to my family — all teachers! — whose insights have shaped my understanding of education.

— Chad Mills

# Author's Note

These practice tests are designed to imitate the style, format, and content of the practice test published by ERB (the Educational Records Bureau) in *What to Expect on the ISEE*, the only book of official preparation materials released by ERB. Some questions are based on appropriate standards from the National Council of Teachers of Mathematics, which ERB cites as a source of content for the ISEE.

The actual ISEE contains a number of unscored questions on each section. Following the example set by ERB in *What to Expect*, I have not included these unscored questions in this book. Consequently, the tests in this book are slightly shorter than the actual ISEE. The timing for each section has been adjusted accordingly. The charts below give the number of questions and corresponding timings for these practice tests and the actual ISEE.

## Practice tests in this book:

| Section | Number of Questions | Time allotted (minutes) |
|---|---|---|
| Verbal Reasoning | 35 | 17.5 |
| Quantitative Reasoning | 32 | 30 |
| Reading Comprehension | 30 | 30 |
| Mathematics Achievement | 42 | 36 |
| Essay | 1 prompt | 30 |
| | Total Time | 143.5 |

## Actual ISEE:

| Section | Number of Questions | Time allotted (minutes) |
|---|---|---|
| Verbal Reasoning | 40 | 20 |
| Quantitative Reasoning | 37 | 35 |
| Reading Comprehension | 36 | 35 |
| Mathematics Achievement | 47 | 40 |
| Essay | 1 prompt | 30 |
| | Total Time | 160 |

# ISEE
Independent School Entrance Exam

# Practice Test 1

# Answer Sheet

## Verbal Reasoning

| | | | | | |
|---|---|---|---|---|---|
| 1 Ⓐ Ⓑ Ⓒ Ⓓ | 13 Ⓐ Ⓑ Ⓒ Ⓓ | 25 Ⓐ Ⓑ Ⓒ Ⓓ |
| 2 Ⓐ Ⓑ Ⓒ Ⓓ | 14 Ⓐ Ⓑ Ⓒ Ⓓ | 26 Ⓐ Ⓑ Ⓒ Ⓓ |
| 3 Ⓐ Ⓑ Ⓒ Ⓓ | 15 Ⓐ Ⓑ Ⓒ Ⓓ | 27 Ⓐ Ⓑ Ⓒ Ⓓ |
| 4 Ⓐ Ⓑ Ⓒ Ⓓ | 16 Ⓐ Ⓑ Ⓒ Ⓓ | 28 Ⓐ Ⓑ Ⓒ Ⓓ |
| 5 Ⓐ Ⓑ Ⓒ Ⓓ | 17 Ⓐ Ⓑ Ⓒ Ⓓ | 29 Ⓐ Ⓑ Ⓒ Ⓓ |
| 6 Ⓐ Ⓑ Ⓒ Ⓓ | 18 Ⓐ Ⓑ Ⓒ Ⓓ | 30 Ⓐ Ⓑ Ⓒ Ⓓ |
| 7 Ⓐ Ⓑ Ⓒ Ⓓ | 19 Ⓐ Ⓑ Ⓒ Ⓓ | 31 Ⓐ Ⓑ Ⓒ Ⓓ |
| 8 Ⓐ Ⓑ Ⓒ Ⓓ | 20 Ⓐ Ⓑ Ⓒ Ⓓ | 32 Ⓐ Ⓑ Ⓒ Ⓓ |
| 9 Ⓐ Ⓑ Ⓒ Ⓓ | 21 Ⓐ Ⓑ Ⓒ Ⓓ | 33 Ⓐ Ⓑ Ⓒ Ⓓ |
| 10 Ⓐ Ⓑ Ⓒ Ⓓ | 22 Ⓐ Ⓑ Ⓒ Ⓓ | 34 Ⓐ Ⓑ Ⓒ Ⓓ |
| 11 Ⓐ Ⓑ Ⓒ Ⓓ | 23 Ⓐ Ⓑ Ⓒ Ⓓ | 35 Ⓐ Ⓑ Ⓒ Ⓓ |
| 12 Ⓐ Ⓑ Ⓒ Ⓓ | 24 Ⓐ Ⓑ Ⓒ Ⓓ | |

## Quantitative Reasoning

| | | | | | |
|---|---|---|---|---|---|
| 1 Ⓐ Ⓑ Ⓒ Ⓓ | 12 Ⓐ Ⓑ Ⓒ Ⓓ | 23 Ⓐ Ⓑ Ⓒ Ⓓ |
| 2 Ⓐ Ⓑ Ⓒ Ⓓ | 13 Ⓐ Ⓑ Ⓒ Ⓓ | 24 Ⓐ Ⓑ Ⓒ Ⓓ |
| 3 Ⓐ Ⓑ Ⓒ Ⓓ | 14 Ⓐ Ⓑ Ⓒ Ⓓ | 25 Ⓐ Ⓑ Ⓒ Ⓓ |
| 4 Ⓐ Ⓑ Ⓒ Ⓓ | 15 Ⓐ Ⓑ Ⓒ Ⓓ | 26 Ⓐ Ⓑ Ⓒ Ⓓ |
| 5 Ⓐ Ⓑ Ⓒ Ⓓ | 16 Ⓐ Ⓑ Ⓒ Ⓓ | 27 Ⓐ Ⓑ Ⓒ Ⓓ |
| 6 Ⓐ Ⓑ Ⓒ Ⓓ | 17 Ⓐ Ⓑ Ⓒ Ⓓ | 28 Ⓐ Ⓑ Ⓒ Ⓓ |
| 7 Ⓐ Ⓑ Ⓒ Ⓓ | 18 Ⓐ Ⓑ Ⓒ Ⓓ | 29 Ⓐ Ⓑ Ⓒ Ⓓ |
| 8 Ⓐ Ⓑ Ⓒ Ⓓ | 19 Ⓐ Ⓑ Ⓒ Ⓓ | 30 Ⓐ Ⓑ Ⓒ Ⓓ |
| 9 Ⓐ Ⓑ Ⓒ Ⓓ | 20 Ⓐ Ⓑ Ⓒ Ⓓ | 31 Ⓐ Ⓑ Ⓒ Ⓓ |
| 10 Ⓐ Ⓑ Ⓒ Ⓓ | 21 Ⓐ Ⓑ Ⓒ Ⓓ | 32 Ⓐ Ⓑ Ⓒ Ⓓ |
| 11 Ⓐ Ⓑ Ⓒ Ⓓ | 22 Ⓐ Ⓑ Ⓒ Ⓓ | |

## Reading Comprehension

| | | | | | |
|---|---|---|---|---|---|
| 1 Ⓐ Ⓑ Ⓒ Ⓓ | 11 Ⓐ Ⓑ Ⓒ Ⓓ | 21 Ⓐ Ⓑ Ⓒ Ⓓ |
| 2 Ⓐ Ⓑ Ⓒ Ⓓ | 12 Ⓐ Ⓑ Ⓒ Ⓓ | 22 Ⓐ Ⓑ Ⓒ Ⓓ |
| 3 Ⓐ Ⓑ Ⓒ Ⓓ | 13 Ⓐ Ⓑ Ⓒ Ⓓ | 23 Ⓐ Ⓑ Ⓒ Ⓓ |
| 4 Ⓐ Ⓑ Ⓒ Ⓓ | 14 Ⓐ Ⓑ Ⓒ Ⓓ | 24 Ⓐ Ⓑ Ⓒ Ⓓ |
| 5 Ⓐ Ⓑ Ⓒ Ⓓ | 15 Ⓐ Ⓑ Ⓒ Ⓓ | 25 Ⓐ Ⓑ Ⓒ Ⓓ |
| 6 Ⓐ Ⓑ Ⓒ Ⓓ | 16 Ⓐ Ⓑ Ⓒ Ⓓ | 26 Ⓐ Ⓑ Ⓒ Ⓓ |
| 7 Ⓐ Ⓑ Ⓒ Ⓓ | 17 Ⓐ Ⓑ Ⓒ Ⓓ | 27 Ⓐ Ⓑ Ⓒ Ⓓ |
| 8 Ⓐ Ⓑ Ⓒ Ⓓ | 18 Ⓐ Ⓑ Ⓒ Ⓓ | 28 Ⓐ Ⓑ Ⓒ Ⓓ |
| 9 Ⓐ Ⓑ Ⓒ Ⓓ | 19 Ⓐ Ⓑ Ⓒ Ⓓ | 29 Ⓐ Ⓑ Ⓒ Ⓓ |
| 10 Ⓐ Ⓑ Ⓒ Ⓓ | 20 Ⓐ Ⓑ Ⓒ Ⓓ | 30 Ⓐ Ⓑ Ⓒ Ⓓ |

## Mathematics Achievement

| | | | | | |
|---|---|---|---|---|---|
| 1 Ⓐ Ⓑ Ⓒ Ⓓ | 15 Ⓐ Ⓑ Ⓒ Ⓓ | 29 Ⓐ Ⓑ Ⓒ Ⓓ |
| 2 Ⓐ Ⓑ Ⓒ Ⓓ | 16 Ⓐ Ⓑ Ⓒ Ⓓ | 30 Ⓐ Ⓑ Ⓒ Ⓓ |
| 3 Ⓐ Ⓑ Ⓒ Ⓓ | 17 Ⓐ Ⓑ Ⓒ Ⓓ | 31 Ⓐ Ⓑ Ⓒ Ⓓ |
| 4 Ⓐ Ⓑ Ⓒ Ⓓ | 18 Ⓐ Ⓑ Ⓒ Ⓓ | 32 Ⓐ Ⓑ Ⓒ Ⓓ |
| 5 Ⓐ Ⓑ Ⓒ Ⓓ | 19 Ⓐ Ⓑ Ⓒ Ⓓ | 33 Ⓐ Ⓑ Ⓒ Ⓓ |
| 6 Ⓐ Ⓑ Ⓒ Ⓓ | 20 Ⓐ Ⓑ Ⓒ Ⓓ | 34 Ⓐ Ⓑ Ⓒ Ⓓ |
| 7 Ⓐ Ⓑ Ⓒ Ⓓ | 21 Ⓐ Ⓑ Ⓒ Ⓓ | 35 Ⓐ Ⓑ Ⓒ Ⓓ |
| 8 Ⓐ Ⓑ Ⓒ Ⓓ | 22 Ⓐ Ⓑ Ⓒ Ⓓ | 36 Ⓐ Ⓑ Ⓒ Ⓓ |
| 9 Ⓐ Ⓑ Ⓒ Ⓓ | 23 Ⓐ Ⓑ Ⓒ Ⓓ | 37 Ⓐ Ⓑ Ⓒ Ⓓ |
| 10 Ⓐ Ⓑ Ⓒ Ⓓ | 24 Ⓐ Ⓑ Ⓒ Ⓓ | 38 Ⓐ Ⓑ Ⓒ Ⓓ |
| 11 Ⓐ Ⓑ Ⓒ Ⓓ | 25 Ⓐ Ⓑ Ⓒ Ⓓ | 39 Ⓐ Ⓑ Ⓒ Ⓓ |
| 12 Ⓐ Ⓑ Ⓒ Ⓓ | 26 Ⓐ Ⓑ Ⓒ Ⓓ | 40 Ⓐ Ⓑ Ⓒ Ⓓ |
| 13 Ⓐ Ⓑ Ⓒ Ⓓ | 27 Ⓐ Ⓑ Ⓒ Ⓓ | 41 Ⓐ Ⓑ Ⓒ Ⓓ |
| 14 Ⓐ Ⓑ Ⓒ Ⓓ | 28 Ⓐ Ⓑ Ⓒ Ⓓ | 42 Ⓐ Ⓑ Ⓒ Ⓓ |

# Answer Sheet - Essay

Write your response in blue or black pen.

STUDENT NAME _____

| Write your essay topic here. |
| :---: |
| _____ |
| _____ |
| _____ |

Write your response here.

_____

_____

_____

_____

_____

_____

_____

_____

_____

_____

_____

_____

_____

_____

_____

_____

_____

_____

_____

_____

_____

_____

_____

_____

_____

_____

(Answer Sheet - Essay continued)

# ISEE

Independent School Entrance Exam

# Upper Level
# Verbal Reasoning

# Practice Test 1

*This page intentionally left blank.*

# Section 1
# Verbal Reasoning

| **35 Questions** | **Time: 17.5 minutes** |

This section is divided into two parts that contain two different types of questions. As soon as you have completed Part One, answer the questions in Part Two. You may write in your test booklet. For each answer you select, fill in the corresponding circle on your answer document.

## Part One — Synonyms

Each question in Part One consists of a word in capital letters followed by four answer choices. Select the one word that is most nearly the same in meaning as the word in capital letters.

| SAMPLE QUESTION: | SAMPLE ANSWER: |
|---|---|
| EXTEND: | Ⓐ ● Ⓒ Ⓓ |
| (A) avoid | |
| (B) lengthen | |
| (C) criticize | |
| (D) discover | |

## Part Two — Sentence Completion

Each question in Part Two is made up of a sentence with one or two blanks. One blank indicates that one word is missing. Two blanks indicate that two words are missing. Each sentence is followed by four answer choices. Select the one word or pair of words that best completes the meaning of the sentence as a whole.

| SAMPLE QUESTIONS: | SAMPLE ANSWERS: |
|---|---|
| Unlike her older brother, who always acted --------, Cheryl preferred to take her time. | ● Ⓑ Ⓒ Ⓓ |
| (A) quickly | |
| (B) carefully | |
| (C) stupidly | |
| (D) wisely | |
| Whitewater rafting is both ------- and dangerous: rapids may provide thrills, but they also threaten a rafter's ------. | Ⓐ Ⓑ Ⓒ ● |
| (A) ancient...pride | |
| (B) understandable...judgment | |
| (C) informative...freedom | |
| (D) exciting...safety | |

STOP. Do not go on until told to do so.    **STOP**

## Part One — Synonyms

**Directions:** Select the word that is most nearly the same in meaning as the word in capital letters.

1. RUBBLE:

   (A) battle
   (B) debris
   (C) pocket
   (D) coinage

2. SURGE:

   (A) deflate
   (B) swell
   (C) attach
   (D) wilt

3. DIRECT:

   (A) frank
   (B) aloof
   (C) popular
   (D) distracted

4. MUTUAL:

   (A) casual
   (B) intimate
   (C) fortunate
   (D) shared

5. DOUSE:

   (A) marry
   (B) ignite
   (C) drench
   (D) capture

6. VALOR:

   (A) courage
   (B) duty
   (C) impression
   (D) expertise

7. ARBITRARY:

   (A) constrained
   (B) groundless
   (C) ethical
   (D) stationary

8. CONSPICUOUS:

   (A) suspicious
   (B) eligible
   (C) obvious
   (D) soothing

9. ENUMERATE:

   (A) correspond
   (B) disregard
   (C) linger
   (D) itemize

10. ACRIMONY:

   (A) payment
   (B) judgment
   (C) willingness
   (D) bitterness

11. FIDELITY:

(A) nationalism
(B) hardship
(C) loyalty
(D) morality

12. DISINTERESTED:

(A) unbiased
(B) restless
(C) routine
(D) guarded

13. SEVER:

(A) retain
(B) dedicate
(C) prolong
(D) cut

14. SAGE:

(A) judicious
(B) fierce
(C) primitive
(D) discouraging

15. IMPLODE:

(A) arrange
(B) collapse
(C) deny
(D) beg

16. SANCTUARY:

(A) religion
(B) artistry
(C) refuge
(D) criticism

17. FORSAKE:

(A) abandon
(B) conclude
(C) embody
(D) pardon

## Part Two — Sentence Completion

**Directions:** Select the word or word pair that best completes the sentence.

18. Human beings crave -------; without such social contact, we lose our sense of purpose and fall into depression.

    (A) wealth
    (B) desire
    (C) companionship
    (D) isolation

19. It is often difficult for a politician to answer reporters' questions without offending his constituents, but the president handled yesterday's press conference with -------.

    (A) anxiety
    (B) aplomb
    (C) aggression
    (D) partisanship

20. University professors are not -------; despite their considerable learning, they make mistakes.

    (A) infallible
    (B) scholarly
    (C) impoverished
    (D) capable

21. As part of a bargain with prosecutors, the criminal agreed to ------- his three brothers as co-conspirators in the robbery.

    (A) pacify
    (B) implicate
    (C) protect
    (D) congratulate

22. Those who live in the poorer favelas of Brazil must endure ------- conditions in which bathrooms are no more than holes in the ground and leaky roofs don't keep out the rain.

    (A) squalid
    (B) hybrid
    (C) tender
    (D) lawless

23. Only the staunchest ------- could appreciate the company's recent production of Macbeth, which followed every established convention.

    (A) reformer
    (B) ambassador
    (C) adherent
    (D) traditionalist

24. Perhaps the world has never seen another
------- quite like the Bubonic Plague, a
terrible contagion that was responsible for
the deaths of millions in the 14<sup>th</sup> century.

(A) parsimony
(B) period
(C) pestilence
(D) scheme

25. Elana has always been an ------- student
who completes all assignments on time and
with meticulous attention to detail.

(A) inefficient
(B) occasional
(C) affable
(D) exemplary

26. After conducting an ------- review of all
studies relevant to milk consumption, the
commission concluded that milk induces
weight gain.

(A) incomplete
(B) elongated
(C) exhaustive
(D) irritating

27. Employers find that it is difficult to
change ------- habits their employees have
developed over many years.

(A) fossilized
(B) ingrained
(C) popular
(D) sluggish

28. The engineers' solution to the bridge's
structural problems was both ------- and
-------; the technique had never been used
before, but it worked very well.

(A) novel…physical
(B) typical…useful
(C) innovative…effective
(D) ingenious…brilliant

29. The cheetah is a ------- predator that never
------- itself until it is very close to its prey.

(A) hungry…disarms
(B) clumsy…unveils
(C) nimble…protects
(D) stealthy…reveals

30. Reports of shark sightings were -------
because they depended on incomplete and
------- testimony.

(A) suspect…contradictory
(B) unreliable…accurate
(C) exaggerated…cautious
(D) frightening…inconsistent

31. That thousands would gather to ------- the
150<sup>th</sup> anniversary of Abraham Lincoln's
Gettysburg Address is a testament to
Lincoln's profound gift for -------.

(A) announce…instruction
(B) survey…tenacity
(C) condemn…reconciliation
(D) commemorate…oratory

32. Facing repeated ------- in his attempt to create the first electric light bulb, Thomas Edison showed great -------, refusing to give up despite the constant setbacks.

    (A) prosperity... resolve
    (B) disappointment...timidity
    (C) failure...determination
    (D) victory...foresight

33. Citizens who value honest, direct communication are disappointed with the governor's recent statements, which are ------- at best; at worst, they are outright -------.

    (A) impenetrable...proclamations
    (B) assertive...vows
    (C) suggestive...revelations
    (D) misleading...falsehoods

34. Artificial intelligence is ------- quickly, and it may ------- human intelligence in the not-too-distant future.

    (A) developing...dodge
    (B) evolving...surpass
    (C) regressing...exceed
    (D) descending...replace

35. The school board wants to overhaul the curriculum -------, while the district's principals support only ------- reform.

    (A) rapidly...incremental
    (B) willfully...deliberate
    (C) temporarily...amicable
    (D) casually...deceptive

12

STOP. Do not go on
until told to do so.

**STOP**

# ISEE

Independent School Entrance Exam

# Upper Level
# Quantitative Reasoning

# Practice Test 1

# Section 2
# Quantitative Reasoning

This section has two parts that contain two different kinds of questions. Do not pause after Part One. Continue working through Part Two. You may write in your test booklet.

Letters such as $x$ and $y$ stand for real numbers. All figures are drawn to scale unless otherwise stated.

**Part One — Word Problems**

Each question in Part One consists of a word problem followed by four answer choices. Select the best answer from the four choices given and fill in the corresponding circle on your answer document.

---

EXAMPLE 1:                                                                SAMPLE ANSWER

Ⓐ Ⓑ Ⓒ ●

Which of the following fractions is greater than $\frac{3}{4}$?

(A) $\frac{1}{5}$

(B) $\frac{1}{4}$

(C) $\frac{2}{5}$

(D) $\frac{4}{5}$

The correct answer is $\frac{4}{5}$, so circle D is darkened.

---

*Go on to the next page.* ➡

# QR

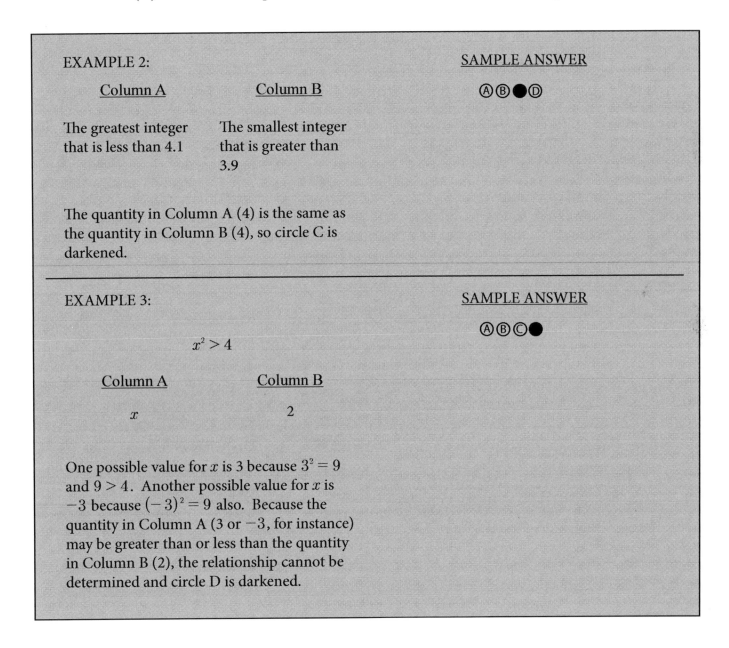

**2**

## Part Two — Quantitative Comparisons

In Part Two, use the given information to compare the quantities given in Column A and Column B.
Choose one of these four answer choices:

        (A)  The quantity in Column A is greater.
        (B)  The quantity in Column B is greater.
        (C)  The two quantities are equal.
        (D)  The relationship cannot be determined from the information given.

---

**EXAMPLE 2:**

      SAMPLE ANSWER

      Ⓐ Ⓑ ● Ⓓ

| Column A | Column B |
|---|---|
| The greatest integer that is less than 4.1 | The smallest integer that is greater than 3.9 |

The quantity in Column A (4) is the same as the quantity in Column B (4), so circle C is darkened.

---

**EXAMPLE 3:**

      SAMPLE ANSWER

      Ⓐ Ⓑ Ⓒ ●

$$x^2 > 4$$

| Column A | Column B |
|---|---|
| $x$ | 2 |

One possible value for $x$ is 3 because $3^2 = 9$ and $9 > 4$. Another possible value for $x$ is $-3$ because $(-3)^2 = 9$ also. Because the quantity in Column A (3 or $-3$, for instance) may be greater than or less than the quantity in Column B (2), the relationship cannot be determined and circle D is darkened.

STOP. Do not go on until told to do so. **STOP**

## Part One — Word Problems

**Directions:** Choose the best answer from the four choices given.

1. Five girls ran a race. The mean time it took the girls to finish the race was 10 minutes and 24 seconds. What was the sum of the girls' times? (Note: there are 60 seconds in one minute)

   (A) 50 minutes
   (B) 51 minutes
   (C) 52 minutes
   (D) 53 minutes

2. If $x$ is an even integer and $y$ is an odd integer, which of the following could NOT be an integer?

   (A) $\frac{xy}{2}$

   (B) $\frac{2y}{x}$

   (C) $\frac{x}{2} + y$

   (D) $x + \frac{y}{2}$

3. What is the sum of the distinct prime factors of 24?

   (A) 10
   (B) 9
   (C) 6
   (D) 5

4. In a tournament, there are three teams: Team A, Team B, and Team C. The three teams will place first, second and third in the tournament, but not necessarily in that order. All possible orderings for the three teams are equally likely. Which of the following events has the lowest probability?

   (A) Team A places first
   (B) Team A places first or Team B places first
   (C) Team A places first and Team B places second
   (D) Team A places first or Team B places second

5. Allen and Drew both work summer jobs that last the same number of weeks. Allen makes $100 more than Drew each week. Which of the following would be needed to determine how much more money Allen makes than Drew over the course of the summer?

   (A) The length of the two summer jobs in weeks
   (B) Drew's salary in dollars per week
   (C) Allen's salary in dollars per week
   (D) The sum of Drew and Allen's salaries in dollars per week

6. Triangle *ABC* is similar to triangle *DEF*. The length of $\overline{AB}$ is 8 inches and the length of $\overline{DE}$ is 20 inches. If the perimeter of triangle *ABC* is 18 inches, what is the perimeter of triangle *DEF*?

(A) 30 inches
(B) 40 inches
(C) 45 inches
(D) 54 inches

7. If $\frac{2x}{5} + \frac{4y}{3}$ is equivalent to $\frac{6x+by}{15}$, what is the value of *b*?

(A) 60
(B) 20
(C) 12
(D) 4

8. The sum of two positive integers is 22. What is the greatest possible difference between the integers?

(A) 19
(B) 20
(C) 21
(D) 22

9. A doctor kept track of the number of times a patient coughs each day for a week. One day during the week, the doctor administered a drug that helps to stop coughing. The drug takes effect three days after it is administered. On which day of the week did the doctor most likely administer the drug?

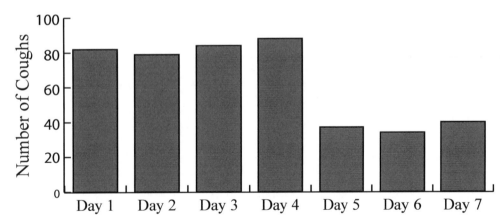

(A) Day 1
(B) Day 2
(C) Day 3
(D) Day 4

10. The frequency bar chart below represents the number of points scored by 14 players on a basketball team during a game.

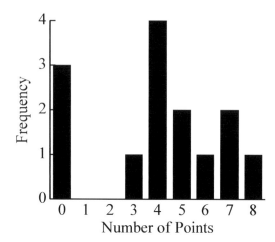

Number of Points

Michelle scored 3 points fewer than Jaclyn, who scored the most points. How many players scored more points than Michelle but fewer points than Jaclyn?

(A) 3
(B) 4
(C) 5
(D) 6

11. If the product of all of the integers from 1 to 100 (inclusive) is $z$, which of the following is an expression for the product of all integers from 1 to 98 (inclusive) in terms of $z$?

(A) $\dfrac{z}{99 \times 100}$
(B) $99 \times z$
(C) $99 \times 100 \times z$
(D) $\dfrac{z}{100}$

12. Mr. Lee's mathematics class of 30 students takes a test. The mean of the scores is 78 and the range of the scores is 31. Afterwards, Mr. Lee decides that the scores are too far apart from each other, so he subtracts 2 from each of the 5 highest scores and adds 2 to each of the 5 lowest scores. What happens to the mean and the range of the scores?

(A) The mean of the scores decreases by 2 and the range decreases by 4
(B) The mean of the scores decreases by 10 and the range decreases by 20
(C) The mean of the scores is unchanged and the range decreases by 2
(D) The mean of the scores is unchanged and the range decreases by 4

13. What is the maximum value for $y$ if $y = \dfrac{1}{x}$ and $-1 \le x \le 1$?

(A) 1
(B) 2
(C) 3
(D) There is no maximum value for $y$

14. If $4x - y = z - 2y$, which of the following expresses $y$ in terms of $z$ and $x$?

(A) $z - 4x$
(B) $4x + z$
(C) $\dfrac{4x - z}{3}$
(D) $4x - z + 3$

15. A large bag of apples contains 50% more apples than a small bag. May has three large bags of apples, and Bill has five small bags of apples. Which of the following is true?

   (A) May and Bill have the same number of apples
   (B) Bill has 20% fewer apples than May
   (C) Bill has 10% fewer apples than May
   (D) May has 10% fewer apples than Bill

16. What is the value of the following expression?
$$\frac{7(7 \times 50 + 7 \times 10)}{49}$$

   (A) $\frac{60}{7}$

   (B) 60

   (C) 120

   (D) 360

Types of Books in a Library by Percentage of Total Books

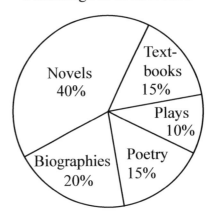

17. The circle graph above represents the percentages of different types of books in a library. The library contains 6000 books. Novels, plays and poetry are considered fiction. All other books are considered non-fiction. Approximately how many non-fiction books are there in the library?

   (A) 3900
   (B) 2100
   (C) 1200
   (D) 900

18. Two different views of the same cube are shown.

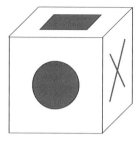 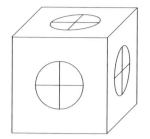

Which of the following could be a different view of the same cube?

(A)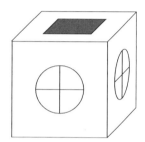

(B)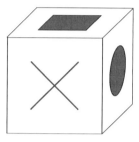

(C)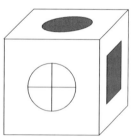

(D)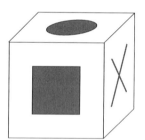

**Part Two—Quantitative Comparisons**

**Directions:** Using the information given in each question, compare the quantity in Column A to the quantity in Column B. All questions in Part Two have these answer choices:

(A)   The quantity in Column A is greater.
(B)   The quantity in Column B is greater.
(C)   The two quantities are equal.
(D)   The relationship cannot be determined from the information given.

---

|   | Column A | Column B |
|---|----------|----------|
| 19. | $x^{4+1}$ | $x^4 + 1$ |

---

A bag contains 10 marbles: 6 red and 4 blue. Of the red marbles, 5 are large and 1 is small. Of the blue marbles, 3 are large and 1 is small. One marble is drawn randomly from the bag.

|   | Column A | Column B |
|---|----------|----------|
| 20. | If a red marble is drawn, the probability that it is large. | If a blue marble is drawn, the probability that it is large. |

---

A balloon is released from a point on the ground and rises straight upward at a rate of 3 feet per second. 10 seconds later, a second balloon is released from the same point and rises straight upward at a rate of 2 feet per second.

|   | Column A | Column B |
|---|----------|----------|
| 21. | The distance between the balloons when the second balloon has been rising for 5 seconds | The distance between the balloons when the second balloon has been rising for 6 seconds |

---

A box contains 20 metal rods, some long and some short. Each long rod weighs 30 grams and each short rod weighs 10 grams. The rods in the box weigh 360 grams all together.

|   | Column A | Column B |
|---|----------|----------|
| 22. | The number of short rods in the box | The number of long rods in the box |

---

Line $q$ is the graph of $x + 3y = 6$. Line $r$ is perpendicular to line $q$.

|   | Column A | Column B |
|---|----------|----------|
| 23. | The slope of line $r$ | 3 |

---

|   | Column A | Column B |
|---|----------|----------|
| 24. | $(x - 5) \times 2$ | $x - 5 \times 2$ |

---

**Answer choices for all questions on this page:**

(A) The quantity in Column A is greater.
(B) The quantity in Column B is greater.
(C) The two quantities are equal.
(D) The relationship cannot be determined from the information given.

A bowl contains 10 slips of paper. Each slip has a different name written on it. Shelly and Bart are two of the names. A slip of paper is drawn from the bowl, then it is replaced and a second slip is drawn.

|  | Column A | Column B |
|---|---|---|
| 25. | The probability that Shelly is drawn both times | The probability that Shelly is drawn first and Bart is drawn second |

$$1 < a < b < c < d$$

|  | Column A | Column B |
|---|---|---|
| 26. | $\dfrac{b}{a} + \dfrac{d}{c}$ | $\dfrac{d+b}{ac}$ |

Dorrell makes a list of 5 consecutive integers, starting at $x$.

|  | Column A | Column B |
|---|---|---|
| 27. | The sum of the five consecutive integers | $5x + 5$ |

$$x < 0$$

|  | Column A | Column B |
|---|---|---|
| 28. | $(x+5)(x+5)$ | $x^2 + 5^2$ |

The value of a stock in the Timber Company increases by 25% from Monday to Tuesday, then decreases by 20% from Tuesday to Wednesday.

|  | Column A | Column B |
|---|---|---|
| 29. | The value of a stock in the Timber Company on Monday | The value of a stock in the Timber Company on Wednesday |

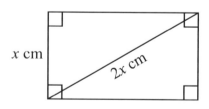

|  | Column A | Column B |
|---|---|---|
| 30. | The perimeter of the rectangle | $6x$ |

**Answer choices for all questions on this page:**

(A) The quantity in Column A is greater.
(B) The quantity in Column B is greater.
(C) The two quantities are equal.
(D) The relationship cannot be determined from the information given.

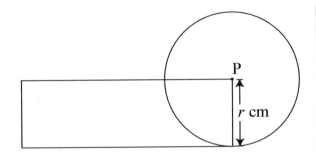

The figure above shows a circle with center P and a rectangle with one vertex at P. The perimeter of the rectangle is $2r + 2\pi r$.

| Column A | Column B |
|----------|----------|
| 31. The area of the circle | The area of the rectangle |

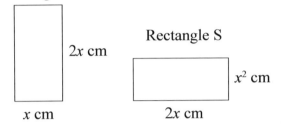

Note: Figures not drawn to scale

| | Column A | Column B |
|---|----------|----------|
| 32. | The perimeter of Rectangle R | The perimeter of Rectangle S |

STOP. If there is time, you may check your work in this section only.

**STOP**

*This page intentionally left blank.*

# ISEE
Independent School Entrance Exam

# Upper Level
# Reading Comprehension

# Practice Test 1

*This page intentionally left blank.*

## Section 3
## Reading Comprehension

This section contains five short reading passages. Each passage is followed by six questions based on its content. Answer the questions following each passage on the basis of what is stated or implied in that passage. You may write in your test booklet.

STOP. Do not go on
until told to do so.

STOP

Questions 1–6

1    Walker has always been the one with the
2  stories: stories of hometown personalities,
3  brushes with fame, chance incidents and
4  accidents, and the quirks of family. Some are
5  comic, others poignant; some are lengthy, others
6  brief. But each of them somehow sheds light on
7  the people who have loomed large in Walker's
8  life and his journey from introverted child to
9  chameleon extraordinaire.
10    His tales are enhanced by his expressive
11  features and a gift for impersonation. His long
12  nose and sharp jaw can become the stern face
13  of his fourth-grade teacher. His soft eyes can
14  evoke his mother's kindliness or his father's
15  pain.  His thin mouth can grow wide with the
16  laughter of children or remain pursed with
17  the wry smiles of old age. One moment, his
18  high cheekbones embody British royalty. The
19  next, they convey the weathered look of a tired
20  fisherman.
21    He tells stories of those he has known since
22  childhood and those whom he has never met.
23  He inhabits both his firsthand and secondhand
24  accounts so completely, though, that one can

25  scarcely tell the difference. Characters from
26  film, television, and the stage slip out of his
27  memory and into casual conversation. He is
28  fluent in children's tales also, and summons up
29  vivid portrayals of the creatures from *Where the
30  Wild Things Are* or the bears from *Goldilocks*,
31  his posture expanding to capture the size and
32  strength of his subject.
33    No character is complete without a voice,
34  and Walker has more voices than a Walt Disney
35  animated feature. His natural tone suggests
36  an aristocratic upbringing, although in truth he
37  came from humble beginnings. He rambles
38  sometimes in the slow drawl of the Bayou or
39  the swallowed mumblings of New England.
40  Shakespeare rolls easily off his tongue, spoken
41  with the fine diction of an accomplished actor.
42  He wheezes and hacks his way through a
43  rendition of an elderly man complaining, then
44  titters off like a little girl. Yet with all of these
45  colors in his palette, perhaps his most effective
46  voice is his own laugh, inviting his listeners to
47  join in the fun.

1. The passage mainly serves to

   (A) reflect on the value of stories
   (B) depict a talented storyteller
   (C) argue that storytelling is underappreciated
   (D) trace a person's upbringing through stories

2. In line 9, the word "chameleon" suggests that Walker is

   (A) very funny
   (B) lizard-like
   (C) adaptable
   (D) emotional

3. The style of the second paragraph (lines 10-20) is mostly characterized by

   (A) tactile description
   (B) extended metaphor
   (C) deliberate exaggeration
   (D) abrupt contrast

4. The passage indicates that Walker might impersonate all of the following EXCEPT

   (A) a nobleman
   (B) someone he doesn't know personally
   (C) someone much younger or older than himself
   (D) the main character of an adult novel

5. The author states that Walker's natural way of speaking

   (A) inspires others to tell stories
   (B) is at odds with his personal background
   (C) suggests he was born in the South
   (D) shows his mother's influence

6. The "colors" referred to in line 45 are different

   (A) characters
   (B) locations
   (C) paints
   (D) situations

Questions 7–12

1　　Even those who don't study wolves may
2　be familiar with the term "alpha wolf." The
3　phrase has long since left zoological circles and
4　entered the common lexicon, where it summons
5　the image of an unusually dominant individual,
6　a person of particular social prominence or
7　stature. It also underlies the popular conception
8　of a wolf pack in the wild—its members
9　squabbling to determine an order amongst
10　themselves, with the strongest or fiercest animal
11　emerging as the "alpha," the leader of the pack.
12　　This establishment of the social strata
13　of a wild wolf pack was long the prevailing
14　viewpoint among scientists. It was believed
15　that packs formed when unrelated wolves
16　banded together in the harshness of winter
17　and subsequently sparred to establish a social
18　hierarchy. Observations of wolves in captivity
19　suggested that the "alpha male" and his mate,
20　the "alpha female," would serve as the only
21　breeding pair in a pack, while more subservient
22　wolves, called "betas" or "omegas," would
23　help to protect and care for the alphas' pups.
24　This view was perpetuated by prominent wolf
25　expert L. David Mech's 1970 book *The Wolf:*
26　*The Ecology and Behavior of an Endangered*
27　*Species.*
28　　Subsequent research, however, has proven
29　these beliefs to be misguided. In 1999, Mech

30　published a paper in the *Canadian Journal*
31　*of Zoology* admitting that the popularly-held
32　view of an "alpha pair" establishing dominance
33　over an unrelated collective was based on
34　behaviors exhibited in captivity and not in the
35　wild. Further observation of wild wolves in
36　their natural habitat suggested that packs are
37　actually biological family groups, composed
38　of a breeding pair and their offspring (usually
39　five to eleven animals total). Young wolves
40　typically stay with the family pack for up to 54
41　months before they disperse, often prompted
42　by sexual maturity or a scarcity of food. Upon
43　leaving their respective family units, unrelated
44　males and females will couple to create their
45　own packs, thus beginning the cycle anew.
46　　Although sometimes two or three families
47　will merge to form a larger pack, it is highly
48　unusual for wild wolves to absorb a stranger
49　into the group—interlopers are usually killed,
50　with rare exception. This of course stands in
51　dramatic contrast to the earlier belief that packs
52　were almost exclusively formed in this way.
53　The disparity between the social constructs
54　of wild and captive wolves speaks to the
55　importance of observing animals in their natural
56　habitats—and to the remarkable adaptability
57　exhibited by such creatures when captivity
58　precludes their natural behaviors.

7. The author would most likely approve of which animal research method?

   (A) designing a maze for mice to solve
   (B) observing wild birds migrating south
   (C) relocating tigers from Africa to Asia
   (D) breeding horses on a farm

8. Which best describes the relationship between the second paragraph (lines 12-27) and the third paragraph (lines 28-45)? The third paragraph

   (A) adds supporting details to the second paragraph
   (B) questions the credibility of scientists mentioned in the second paragraph
   (C) corrects a misconception discussed in the second paragraph
   (D) explains why wolves behave as described in the second paragraph

9. As used in line 4, "lexicon" most nearly means

   (A) company
   (B) classification
   (C) vocabulary
   (D) discussion

10. In captivity, wolf packs mostly consist of

    (A) unrelated wolves
    (B) biological family units
    (C) wolves of the same age
    (D) orphaned wolves

11. In the wild, a new wolf pack often forms when

    (A) many individual wolves band together
    (B) two wolves from the same pack leave together
    (C) an unrelated wolf joins a pack
    (D) two wolves from different packs mate

12. The author views the term "alpha wolf" as

    (A) inconsistent
    (B) obscure
    (C) useful
    (D) misleading

Questions 13–18

1     The renowned art collection assembled
2 over thirty years by Dorothy and Herbert Vogel
3 has been called "one of the most remarkable
4 American collections formed in the twentieth
5 century, one that covers most of the important
6 developments in contemporary art." Two civil
7 servants by profession with no independent
8 financial means, the Vogels have acquired some
9 four thousand objects, primarily drawings. In
10 the early years of their collecting journey, the
11 Vogels provided moral and modest financial
12 support to a number of relatively unknown
13 artists who subsequently received international
14 acclaim. Among them were Robert Barry, Sol
15 LeWitt, Edda Renouf, and Richard Tuttle, all
16 of whom became close friends of the Vogels.
17 By the 1970s, when the work of these and
18 other artists represented in the Vogel Collection
19 became widely exhibited and recognized by
20 the international art press, Dorothy and Herbert
21 likewise were acknowledged for their early,
22 prescient attention to the work.
23     As is the case for many collectors,
24 the Vogels initially set out not to build "a
25 collection" per se, but rather to acquire works
26 they admired and wanted for their home. The art
27 community's awareness of the limited funds
28 the couple could devote to these acquisitions
29 brought the Vogels considerable admiration,
30 as did their enthusiastic response to a range of
31 contemporary work that many collectors found
32 difficult to appreciate—new forms employing
33 non-traditional materials such as latex, string,
34 and Styrofoam. Most frequently referred
35 to as collectors of minimal and conceptual
36 art, the Vogels always had a more expansive
37 reach. They collected art rooted in abstract
38 expressionism, as exemplified by Michael
39 Goldberg and Charles Clough; innovative
40 post-minimalist approaches, as seen in the art
41 of Richard Francisco and Pat Steir; and diverse
42 figurative directions, such as that embraced by
43 Will Barnet and Mark Kostabe, among others.
44     The Vogels donated their collection to the
45 National Gallery of Art in 1992, in part because
46 of the Gallery's commitment to free admission
47 to its exhibits. In 2008, they again partnered
48 with the National Gallery of Art to launch a
49 program that distributed 2,500 works of art
50 to museums across the fifty states, promoting
51 broad access to contemporary art in the process.

13. The author demonstrates the variety of art the Vogels purchased by

    (A) citing particular artists whose works they own
    (B) referring to them as collectors of minimal and conceptual art
    (C) stating that they donated works to museums in fifty states
    (D) focusing on their civil service

14. The passage indicates that the Vogels achieved recognition because they

    (A) supported important artists before those artists became famous
    (B) spent more money on art than other collectors
    (C) kept their artwork in their home
    (D) only purchased drawings

15. It can be inferred from the passage that the Vogels believed

    (A) non-traditional artwork is better than traditional artwork
    (B) artists and collectors should not be friends
    (C) art should be accessible to a wide range of people
    (D) art belongs in museums, not in private homes

16. The primary purpose of the passage is to

    (A) praise artists for creative use of new materials
    (B) acquaint the reader with two art enthusiasts and their collection
    (C) detail how the Vogel collection became widely exhibited
    (D) explain the motivation for an act of charity

17. The passage indicates that Charles Clough

    (A) used a post-minimalist approach
    (B) was an abstract expressionist
    (C) was a friend of the Vogels
    (D) was aware of the Vogels' limited funds

18. The author of the passage cites "latex, string, and Styrofoam" (lines 33-34) as examples of materials that were

    (A) used in minimalist, conceptual art
    (B) not respected by many collectors
    (C) not very durable
    (D) affordable for artists with limited funds

Questions 19–24

1  Sandy watched the clock above the doors
2  anxiously. It was three o'clock, and the matches
3  were scheduled to begin at 2:45. There was still
4  no word from the organizers, though, and he sat
5  with the other hopefuls in the cafeteria-turned-
6  waiting room, trying his best not to sweat.
7      It was a losing battle. His hands were
8  clammy, and a telltale sheen appeared on his
9  forehead. This would be his first tournament
10  since starting chess lessons, and Father had high
11  expectations. Father himself had been a junior
12  champion, as he constantly reminded anyone at
13  the tournament who cared to listen. The other
14  parents nodded politely, but Sandy noticed that
15  none of them spoke with Father for very long.
16      The short blond girl at the neighboring table
17  peered at Sandy curiously. She was younger
18  than Sandy by a year or two, and her glasses
19  magnified her eyes, adding accidental intensity
20  to her stare. He hadn't seen her before, and the
21  directness of her attention made him uneasy. He
22  looked down at his hands, then at the clock,

23  then back to his hands. They were damper than
24  before. When he patted them on the sleeves
25  of his shirt, dark marks of moisture remained
26  behind on the fabric. Embarrassed, he tried to
27  roll up his sleeves, only to find that his cuff links
28  were too tight.
29      He sat back, defeated, folding his hands on
30  the table in front of him. The soft ticking sound
31  of the clock above the door drifted through the
32  room. One boy by the window had a cold, and
33  his occasional sniffle echoed off the tile floor.
34  Sandy closed his eyes. Perspiration dripped
35  from his eyebrow to his cheek. He waited for
36  the muffled click of the double doors opening.
37      Instead of the click, he felt a tap on his
38  arm. He turned and saw no one above his
39  shoulder, then looked down into those bug-
40  eyes that had been watching him from the other
41  table. The blond girl was holding up a piece of
42  cloth. It took Sandy a moment to understand: a
43  handkerchief. She had come to his rescue.

19. After recognizing the handkerchief, Sandy most likely feels

    (A) confused
    (B) nervous
    (C) grateful
    (D) insulted

20. That author implies that the "other parents" (lines 13-14)

    (A) feel threatened by Sandy
    (B) are too busy to talk
    (C) dislike Father's conversation
    (D) have neglected their own children

21. It can be inferred from the passage that the cafeteria is

    (A) quiet
    (B) crowded
    (C) poorly lit
    (D) uncomfortably warm

22. Sandy is bothered by all of the following EXCEPT

    (A) the late start of the tournament
    (B) the direct attention of the blond girl
    (C) dark patches of moisture on his sleeves
    (D) the blond girl's tap on his arm

23. Sandy is anxious because he

    (A) has never played chess before
    (B) is aware of Father's expectations
    (C) has only been taking lessons a short time
    (D) wants to impress the blonde girl

24. The author describes Sandy as "defeated" (line 29) because Sandy

    (A) feels he has already lost the tournament
    (B) can't return the blonde girl's stare
    (C) is unable to accomplish a task
    (D) has decided not to compete

Questions 25–30

Following a recent concert by a young,
dynamic pianist, a scathing review appeared in a
national paper. Too much motion, declared the
reviewer. Too much freedom. Too much license
with the original material. The pianist, in the
pundit's esteemed opinion, had spent the whole
evening satisfying his own desires and ignoring
the demands of the music on the page. This
self-absorbed upstart served his own purposes
rather than the purposes of the composer,
Ludwig van Beethoven.

It's no wonder that the public at large
thinks of classical music as stuffy and out of
touch. Purists insist that we must respect the
composer's intent, that we must play the notes
exactly as written on the page, following the
tempo indications and dynamic markings as laid
out by the giants of centuries past. A modern
performer who chooses to deviate from the
score is accused of impertinence, presuming
that she knows better than the composer himself
how the music should be interpreted.

The purists' attitude is summarized by the
simple assertion that as musicians, we must
serve the music. But why not take the opposite
perspective? Why shouldn't the music serve
us? We—pianists or singers, children or adults,
amateurs or professionals—make music to
satisfy our own desires and aspirations, not
to serve some abstract, distant authority. All
agree that Beethoven was a genius, but even so,
the man has been dead for nearly two hundred
years. What he wrote served him in his time.
We still draw inspiration from it today. But our
response to Beethoven's genius must remain
exactly that: inspiration to create our own art,
not slavish imitation of his.

Corporations, classical music's benefactors
in the era of declining revenue from sales of
tickets and recordings, contribute to the
problem of excessive reverence for the great
works and their authors. With their generous
financial support, sponsors buy a piece of the
mystical high-culture cachet that accompanies
performances of Wagner at the Metropolitan
Opera or Mozart at the Berlin Philharmonic. By
associating with brand-name composers and
institutions in classical music, these companies
polish their own brands. Naturally, then, they
contribute to lavish marketing campaigns
emphasizing the great historical traditions of the
works. In the process, they enhance the image
of the composer as the all-knowing master, a
prophet of music whose revelations we mortals
cannot question.

There is a deeper impulse, though, that
drives us to faithfully replicate the composer's
intent. It is the same impulse that drives
families across the country to drag trees into
their homes in December and eat turkey on
Thanksgiving: tradition. We instinctually
participate in the rituals we have grown up with
because they are what we know. They connect
us to our past, our ancestors, our cultural
inheritance. We are comforted by the continuity
that tradition provides. By playing Beethoven
the way that our great-grandparents might have,
we affirm our place in the historical chain.

It is only natural, then, that purists cling
to the established patterns of the past. But in
so doing, they risk becoming irrelevant. Even
our most cherished traditions change and grow
over time. Music has changed dramatically in
the past century or two, and although there is
still a place for symphonies and sonatas in our
world, a narrow-minded concept of correctness
is pushing classical music ever further to the
margins of popular art.

25. The primary argument of the passage is that

(A) great composers should be honored

(B) classical music is becoming less popular

(C) too much respect for musical tradition is a bad thing

(D) corporate influence is corrupting music

26. The author describes the scathing music review (lines 2-11) in order to illustrate

(A) a narrow-minded perspective on music

(B) how a performance can go wrong

(C) the dangers of too much emotion in music

(D) the immaturity of today's young musicians

27. It can be inferred from the third paragraph (lines 23-37) that the author

(A) doesn't enjoy Beethoven's music

(B) considers many different kinds of people musicians

(C) thinks classical music is uninteresting

(D) believes musicians must serve the music

28. In lines 52 to 55 ("In the process... question") the author makes use of

(A) religious imagery

(B) comic irony

(C) understatement

(D) direct comparison

29. According to the passage, corporations sponsor classical music because of

(A) effective marketing campaigns

(B) selfless generosity

(C) reverence for great composers

(D) a desire for good publicity

30. According to the last paragraph (lines 69-78), the desire to follow musical traditions is

(A) boring

(B) correct

(C) elitist

(D) natural

STOP. If there is time, you may check your work on this section only.

STOP

*This page intentionally left blank.*

# ISEE

Independent School Entrance Exam

# Upper Level
# Mathematics Achievement

# Practice Test 1

*This page intentionally left blank.*

**4**

## Section 4
## Mathematics Achievement

42 Questions

Time: 36 minutes

Choose the best answer from the four choices given. Fill in the corresponding circle on your answer document. You may write in the test booklet.

SAMPLE QUESTION:

What number is 40% of 50?

(A) 10
(B) 20
(C) 30
(D) 40

The correct answer is 20, so circle B is darkened.

SAMPLE ANSWER

Ⓐ ● Ⓒ Ⓓ

STOP. Do not go on until told to do so.

**STOP**

1. Which value is equal to $\pi$?

   (A) $\dfrac{22}{7}$

   (B) 3.14

   (C) $\dfrac{3\pi - \pi}{2}$

   (D) $2 \times \sqrt{3}$

2. Which expression is equivalent to the expression $2x^2 - (x + 3x^2)$?

   (A) $-x^2 - x$
   (B) $5x^2 - x$
   (C) $-2x^2$
   (D) $5x^2$

3. If $3(2 - y) = 6(y + 1)$, which of the following is the value of $y$?

   (A) 0

   (B) $\dfrac{1}{2}$

   (C) 2

   (D) there are no values of $y$ that make the equation true

4. There are 40 people on a bus: 10 teachers and 30 students. The average height of the students is 50 inches. If the average height of all the people on the bus is 55 inches, what is the average height of the teachers?

   (A) 58 inches
   (B) 60 inches
   (C) 65 inches
   (D) 70 inches

5. The grid below consists of identical rectangles and an irregularly shaped shaded region. The total area of the grid is 96 inches$^2$.

   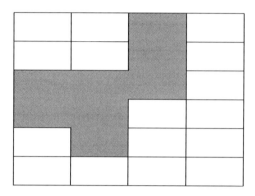

   What is the area of the shaded region?

   (A) 32 inches$^2$
   (B) 36 inches$^2$
   (C) 40 inches$^2$
   (D) 48 inches$^2$

6. A jar contains 17 marbles. 8 are red, 7 are green, and the remainder are blue. Three marbles are randomly removed from the jar, and none of the marbles are returned to the jar before selecting the next marble. What is the probability that at least one marble is NOT blue?

   (A) $\dfrac{15}{17} \times \dfrac{14}{16} \times \dfrac{13}{15}$

   (B) $1 - \dfrac{15}{17} \times \dfrac{14}{16} \times \dfrac{13}{15}$

   (C) $1 - \dfrac{2}{17}$

   (D) 1

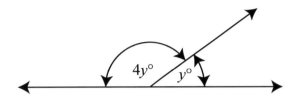

7. For what values of $x$ does $\dfrac{x^2-49}{(x+7)} = 0$ ?

   (A) $x = -7$ only
   (B) $x = 7$ only
   (C) $x = -7$ and $x = 7$
   (D) There are no real values of $x$ for which the equation is true

8. A congressman from Texas receives 40 letters from Texans in support of a piece of legislation and 60 letters from Texans opposing the legislation. Of the following conclusions, which is best justified by this data?

   (A) Most Texans oppose the legislation.
   (B) Most Texans who oppose the legislation wrote letters to the congressman.
   (C) Most Texans who wrote letters to the congressman oppose the legislation.
   (D) Most people who oppose the legislation are Texans.

9. If $x$ is a positive number, which expression is equivalent to $\sqrt{9x^{36}}$ ?

   (A) $3x^{36}$
   (B) $3x^{18}$
   (C) $9x^{36}$
   (D) $9x^{18}$

10. Which gives all values of $x$ for which $|x+1|+3 > 3$?

    (A) $-1$
    (B) all real values of $x$
    (C) all real values of $x$ except $-1$
    (D) there are no real values of $x$ that make the equation true

11. In the figure above, what is the value of $y$?

    (A) 45
    (B) 36
    (C) 22.5
    (D) 18

12. $x$ is the greatest common factor of $10ab^3$ and $4a^2b$.

    $y$ is the least common multiple of $10ab^3$ and $4a^2b$.

    Which of the following is equal to $\dfrac{y}{x}$?

    (A) $10ab^2$
    (B) $20ab^2$
    (C) $10a^2b^3$
    (D) $20ab$

13. Points $(-4,0)$ and $(2,-8)$ are the endpoints of a diameter of a circle. What is the radius of the circle?

    (A) 4
    (B) 5
    (C) 6
    (D) 10

14. A building that is 20 meters high casts an 8 meter shadow on the ground, as shown in the diagram.

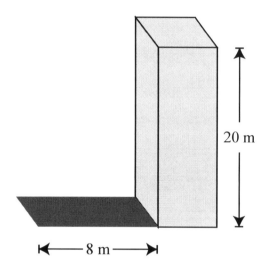

At the same time, Ashton stands next to the building in the sunlight. If Ashton is 4 feet tall, how long is Ashton's shadow on the ground?

(A) 1.5 feet
(B) 1.6 feet
(C) 1.7 feet
(D) 1.8 feet

15. If $-a(1-b) = -(ab + a)$, which of the following must be true?

(A) $a = 0$
(B) $a = 0$ and $b = 0$
(C) $a = 0$ or $b = 0$
(D) there are no real values of a and b that make the equation true

16. Josiah researched the number of professional sports teams in each of 10 large cities. His data is shown on the bar chart below.

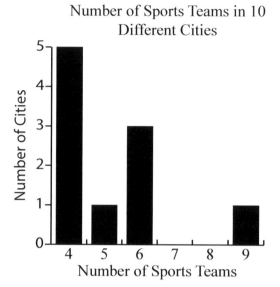

What is the mean number of professional sports teams in the 10 cities that Josiah researched?

(A) 5.1
(B) 5.2
(C) 5.5
(D) 6.0

17. Which of the following expressions represents an irrational number?

(A) $\sqrt{121}$
(B) $\sqrt{2} \times \sqrt{2}$
(C) $\sqrt{18} \times \sqrt{2}$
(D) $\sqrt{9} \times \sqrt{2}$

18. The following table shows the number of students who received each of 5 possible grades on a test.

| Grade | Number of students who received that grade |
|-------|--------------------------------------------|
| 100   | 4                                          |
| 90    | 13                                         |
| 80    | 5                                          |
| 70    | 11                                         |
| 60    | 12                                         |

How many students received a grade higher than the mode?

(A) 4
(B) 13
(C) 17
(D) 22

19. The box-and-whisker plot below shows the fuel efficiency, in miles per gallon, of 100 automobiles.

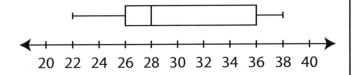

20  22  24  26  28  30  32  34  36  38  40

Approximately 75% of the automobiles have a fuel efficiency less than what value?

(A) 36 miles per gallon
(B) 34 miles per gallon
(C) 32 miles per gallon
(D) 30 miles per gallon

20. What is the value of the numerical expression $(\sqrt{18} + \sqrt{2})^2$?

(A) 20
(B) 32
(C) 34
(D) 400

21. A factory produces wooden posts. The weight of the posts increases by a constant amount for each increase of 1 foot in the height of the posts.

| Height (feet)   | 8 | 10 | 12 | 14 | 16 |
|-----------------|---|----|----|----|----|
| Weight (pounds) | $x$ | 15 | 18 | $y$ | 24 |

What is the value of $y - x$?

(A) 9
(B) 10
(C) 11
(D) 12

22. Which expression is equivalent to $x^2 - 2x - 15$?

(A) $(x - 2)(x + 15)$
(B) $(x - 2)(x - 15)$
(C) $(x - 5)(x + 3)$
(D) $(x + 5)(x - 3)$

23. The grid below shows 3 vertices of a trapezoid.

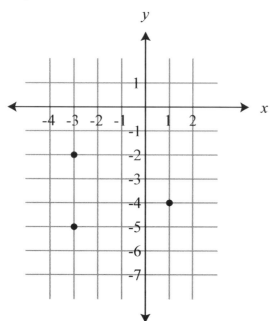

Which of the following could be the fourth vertex of the trapezoid?

(A) $(1, -1)$
(B) $(0, -2)$
(C) $(-1, -1)$
(D) $(-1, -6)$

24. $\dfrac{2 \times 10^{-2} - 2 \times 10^{-3}}{3} =$

(A) $0$
(B) $6 \times 10^{-4}$
(C) $6 \times 10^{-3}$
(D) $6 \times 10^{-2}$

25. Which is the most reasonable unit for measuring the speed of a person riding a bicycle?

(A) feet per day
(B) square centimeters per second
(C) meters per second
(D) centimeters per hour

26. The following stem-and-leaf plot represents the ages in years of swimmers at a pool.

| Stem | Leaf | | | | | |
|------|---|---|---|---|---|---|
| 1 | 2 | 5 | 7 | | | |
| 2 | 3 | 3 | 6 | 8 | 9 | 9 |
| 3 | 0 | 1 | 3 | 4 | | |
| 4 | 3 | 4 | 7 | | | |
| 5 | 0 | 6 | 6 | 7 | 7 | 7 |
| 6 | 1 | 3 | | | | |

What is the range of the swimmers' ages?

(A) 33.5 years
(B) 51.0 years
(C) 57.0 years
(D) 63.0 years

27. A solution set is graphed in the number line shown.

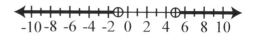

-10 -8 -6 -4 -2 0 2 4 6 8 10

The solution set of which inequality is shown?

(A) $|x - 2| > 3$
(B) $|x - 2| < 3$
(C) $|x + 2| > 3$
(D) $|x + 2| < 3$

28. The graph of line $m$ is shown.

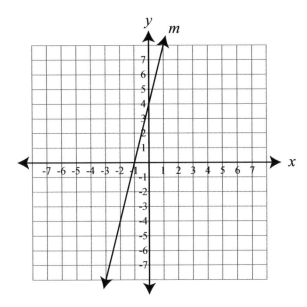

Line $l$ (not shown) is perpendicular to line $m$. What is the slope of line $l$?

(A) $-\dfrac{1}{4}$

(B) 4

(C) $\dfrac{1}{4}$

(D) 4

29. If $5(m-n) = m^2 - n^2$, where $m$ and $n$ are positive integers and $m > n$, which of the following could be the value of $m$?

(A) 2

(B) 3

(C) 5

(D) 6

30. At a pet show, there are three dogs for every two cats. Dogs and cats are the only pets at the show. If there are 75 pets at the show all together, how many dogs are there?

(A) 25

(B) 30

(C) 45

(D) 50

31. There are five members of a student senate. The senate is to elect a president and a vice president from its members. If the president cannot also be the vice president, how many outcomes of the election are possible?

(A) 5

(B) 10

(C) 15

(D) 20

32. In the correctly worked out addition problem below, $A$ and $B$ represent digits.

$$\begin{array}{r} 47 \\ + \quad A \\ \hline B3 \end{array}$$

What is the value of $A + B$?

(A) 7

(B) 10

(C) 11

(D) 14

33. The figure shows a rectangle that measures 6 cm by 1 cm.

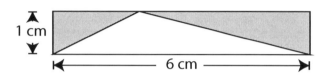

What is the area of the shaded region?

(A) 2 cm²

(B) 3 cm²

(C) 4 cm²

(D) the area of the shaded region cannot be determined from the information given

34. There were 16 students in Ms. Garfield's class at the end of 2009. The number of students in her class decreased by 25% during each of the next two years. How many students were in her class at the end of 2011?

(A) 4

(B) 8

(C) 9

(D) 11

35. The formula for the volume, V, of a cone is $V = \frac{1}{3}\pi r^2 h$, where $r$ is the radius of the cone and $h$ is the height of the cone. If the volume of Cone A is $\frac{9}{8}\pi$ cubic centimeters and the radius of Cone A is equal to its height, what is the radius of Cone A?

(A) $\frac{3}{8}$ centimeters

(B) $\frac{3}{4}$ centimeters

(C) $\frac{9}{16}$ centimeters

(D) $\frac{3}{2}$ centimeters

36. "All prime numbers greater than 13 are one greater than a multiple of four."

Which of the following numbers shows the above statement is FALSE?

(A) 17

(B) 31

(C) 39

(D) 41

37. What is the result of the matrix expression
$3\begin{bmatrix} 1 \\ 4 \end{bmatrix} + 2\begin{bmatrix} 5 \\ 3 \end{bmatrix}$ ?

(A) $\begin{bmatrix} 13 \\ 17 \end{bmatrix}$

(B) $\begin{bmatrix} 30 \\ 60 \end{bmatrix}$

(C) $\begin{bmatrix} 6 \\ 18 \end{bmatrix}$

(D) $\begin{bmatrix} 13 \\ 18 \end{bmatrix}$

38. A bin contains 18 red golf balls and 7 blue golf balls. Penelope randomly selects a golf ball from the bin, plays a round of golf, then returns the ball to the bin. Derek then selects a ball from the bin. If Penelope selects a blue ball, what is the probability that the ball Derek selects is also blue?

(A) $\frac{7}{25}$

(B) $\frac{7}{18}$

(C) $\frac{6}{25}$

(D) $\frac{7}{25} \times \frac{6}{25}$

39. There are 16 ounces in one pound. One gallon of gasoline weighs 97.16 ounces. If a vehicle can travel 30 miles using one gallon of gasoline, which of the following expresses the distance, in miles, that the vehicle can travel using one pound of gasoline?

(A) $\frac{30}{97.16 \times 16}$

(B) $\frac{30 \times 97.16}{16}$

(C) $\frac{97.16}{30 \times 16}$

(D) $\frac{16 \times 30}{97.16}$

40. If $i^2 = -1$, what is the value of $(i+3)(i-3)$?

(A) $-10$

(B) $-8$

(C) $i$

(D) $i-9$

41. In a theater, all seats are organized into rows and each row contains 25 seats. At one performance, all seats were full and 13 people stood in the back. Which of the following could NOT be the total number of people who attended the performance?

(A) 138

(B) 213

(C) 263

(D) 323

42. The bar graph below shows the high and low temperatures for five days last summer.

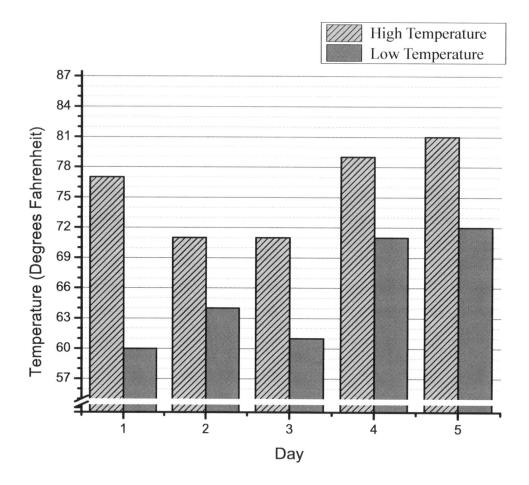

James makes a list of daily temperature ranges by subtracting the low temperature from the high temperature for each of the five days. On which day does the median daily temperature range occur?

(A) Day 1

(B) Day 2

(C) Day 4

(D) Day 5

# Essay Directions

There is an essay topic printed on the next page of this test. Do not turn the page until you are told to begin. Once you are told to begin, you will have 30 minutes to write an essay on the topic provided. You may not write on another topic.

Your writing should be as clear as possible. The quality of your writing is more important than the length of your essay, but your essay should be long enough to develop your ideas and to demonstrate your writing ability.

You may plan your response in the notes section provided on the next page. Any writing you do in the notes section will NOT be counted as part of your essay. Your final draft must be written on the lined portion of your answer sheet. Only what is written on your answer sheet will be considered part of your essay. Remember that you will have only 30 minutes to plan and write your essay, so you should leave enough time to copy your final draft to the answer sheet.

Please use a blue or black pen to write your essay. Do not write outside of the box provided on the answer sheet. You may write in cursive or in print.

Please copy the following topic onto the first few lines of your answer sheet.

# Essay Topic

| **How do you resolve conflicts with other people?  Give one or more examples.** |

- • Do not write on any other topic.
- • Write your final draft on the answer sheet, NOT in the space below.
- • Write in blue or black pen.

## Notes

_____

_____

_____

_____

_____

_____

_____

_____

_____

_____

_____

_____

_____

_____

_____

# ISEE
Independent School Entrance Exam

# Practice Test 2

# Answer Sheet

## Verbal Reasoning

| | | | | | | | | |
|---|---|---|---|---|---|---|---|---|
| 1 | Ⓐ Ⓑ Ⓒ Ⓓ | 13 | Ⓐ Ⓑ Ⓒ Ⓓ | 25 | Ⓐ Ⓑ Ⓒ Ⓓ |
| 2 | Ⓐ Ⓑ Ⓒ Ⓓ | 14 | Ⓐ Ⓑ Ⓒ Ⓓ | 26 | Ⓐ Ⓑ Ⓒ Ⓓ |
| 3 | Ⓐ Ⓑ Ⓒ Ⓓ | 15 | Ⓐ Ⓑ Ⓒ Ⓓ | 27 | Ⓐ Ⓑ Ⓒ Ⓓ |
| 4 | Ⓐ Ⓑ Ⓒ Ⓓ | 16 | Ⓐ Ⓑ Ⓒ Ⓓ | 28 | Ⓐ Ⓑ Ⓒ Ⓓ |
| 5 | Ⓐ Ⓑ Ⓒ Ⓓ | 17 | Ⓐ Ⓑ Ⓒ Ⓓ | 29 | Ⓐ Ⓑ Ⓒ Ⓓ |
| 6 | Ⓐ Ⓑ Ⓒ Ⓓ | 18 | Ⓐ Ⓑ Ⓒ Ⓓ | 30 | Ⓐ Ⓑ Ⓒ Ⓓ |
| 7 | Ⓐ Ⓑ Ⓒ Ⓓ | 19 | Ⓐ Ⓑ Ⓒ Ⓓ | 31 | Ⓐ Ⓑ Ⓒ Ⓓ |
| 8 | Ⓐ Ⓑ Ⓒ Ⓓ | 20 | Ⓐ Ⓑ Ⓒ Ⓓ | 32 | Ⓐ Ⓑ Ⓒ Ⓓ |
| 9 | Ⓐ Ⓑ Ⓒ Ⓓ | 21 | Ⓐ Ⓑ Ⓒ Ⓓ | 33 | Ⓐ Ⓑ Ⓒ Ⓓ |
| 10 | Ⓐ Ⓑ Ⓒ Ⓓ | 22 | Ⓐ Ⓑ Ⓒ Ⓓ | 34 | Ⓐ Ⓑ Ⓒ Ⓓ |
| 11 | Ⓐ Ⓑ Ⓒ Ⓓ | 23 | Ⓐ Ⓑ Ⓒ Ⓓ | 35 | Ⓐ Ⓑ Ⓒ Ⓓ |
| 12 | Ⓐ Ⓑ Ⓒ Ⓓ | 24 | Ⓐ Ⓑ Ⓒ Ⓓ | | |

## Quantitative Reasoning

| | | | | | | | | |
|---|---|---|---|---|---|---|---|---|
| 1 | Ⓐ Ⓑ Ⓒ Ⓓ | 12 | Ⓐ Ⓑ Ⓒ Ⓓ | 23 | Ⓐ Ⓑ Ⓒ Ⓓ |
| 2 | Ⓐ Ⓑ Ⓒ Ⓓ | 13 | Ⓐ Ⓑ Ⓒ Ⓓ | 24 | Ⓐ Ⓑ Ⓒ Ⓓ |
| 3 | Ⓐ Ⓑ Ⓒ Ⓓ | 14 | Ⓐ Ⓑ Ⓒ Ⓓ | 25 | Ⓐ Ⓑ Ⓒ Ⓓ |
| 4 | Ⓐ Ⓑ Ⓒ Ⓓ | 15 | Ⓐ Ⓑ Ⓒ Ⓓ | 26 | Ⓐ Ⓑ Ⓒ Ⓓ |
| 5 | Ⓐ Ⓑ Ⓒ Ⓓ | 16 | Ⓐ Ⓑ Ⓒ Ⓓ | 27 | Ⓐ Ⓑ Ⓒ Ⓓ |
| 6 | Ⓐ Ⓑ Ⓒ Ⓓ | 17 | Ⓐ Ⓑ Ⓒ Ⓓ | 28 | Ⓐ Ⓑ Ⓒ Ⓓ |
| 7 | Ⓐ Ⓑ Ⓒ Ⓓ | 18 | Ⓐ Ⓑ Ⓒ Ⓓ | 29 | Ⓐ Ⓑ Ⓒ Ⓓ |
| 8 | Ⓐ Ⓑ Ⓒ Ⓓ | 19 | Ⓐ Ⓑ Ⓒ Ⓓ | 30 | Ⓐ Ⓑ Ⓒ Ⓓ |
| 9 | Ⓐ Ⓑ Ⓒ Ⓓ | 20 | Ⓐ Ⓑ Ⓒ Ⓓ | 31 | Ⓐ Ⓑ Ⓒ Ⓓ |
| 10 | Ⓐ Ⓑ Ⓒ Ⓓ | 21 | Ⓐ Ⓑ Ⓒ Ⓓ | 32 | Ⓐ Ⓑ Ⓒ Ⓓ |
| 11 | Ⓐ Ⓑ Ⓒ Ⓓ | 22 | Ⓐ Ⓑ Ⓒ Ⓓ | | |

## Reading Comprehension

| | | | | | | | | |
|---|---|---|---|---|---|---|---|---|
| 1 | Ⓐ Ⓑ Ⓒ Ⓓ | 11 | Ⓐ Ⓑ Ⓒ Ⓓ | 21 | Ⓐ Ⓑ Ⓒ Ⓓ |
| 2 | Ⓐ Ⓑ Ⓒ Ⓓ | 12 | Ⓐ Ⓑ Ⓒ Ⓓ | 22 | Ⓐ Ⓑ Ⓒ Ⓓ |
| 3 | Ⓐ Ⓑ Ⓒ Ⓓ | 13 | Ⓐ Ⓑ Ⓒ Ⓓ | 23 | Ⓐ Ⓑ Ⓒ Ⓓ |
| 4 | Ⓐ Ⓑ Ⓒ Ⓓ | 14 | Ⓐ Ⓑ Ⓒ Ⓓ | 24 | Ⓐ Ⓑ Ⓒ Ⓓ |
| 5 | Ⓐ Ⓑ Ⓒ Ⓓ | 15 | Ⓐ Ⓑ Ⓒ Ⓓ | 25 | Ⓐ Ⓑ Ⓒ Ⓓ |
| 6 | Ⓐ Ⓑ Ⓒ Ⓓ | 16 | Ⓐ Ⓑ Ⓒ Ⓓ | 26 | Ⓐ Ⓑ Ⓒ Ⓓ |
| 7 | Ⓐ Ⓑ Ⓒ Ⓓ | 17 | Ⓐ Ⓑ Ⓒ Ⓓ | 27 | Ⓐ Ⓑ Ⓒ Ⓓ |
| 8 | Ⓐ Ⓑ Ⓒ Ⓓ | 18 | Ⓐ Ⓑ Ⓒ Ⓓ | 28 | Ⓐ Ⓑ Ⓒ Ⓓ |
| 9 | Ⓐ Ⓑ Ⓒ Ⓓ | 19 | Ⓐ Ⓑ Ⓒ Ⓓ | 29 | Ⓐ Ⓑ Ⓒ Ⓓ |
| 10 | Ⓐ Ⓑ Ⓒ Ⓓ | 20 | Ⓐ Ⓑ Ⓒ Ⓓ | 30 | Ⓐ Ⓑ Ⓒ Ⓓ |

## Mathematics Achievement

| | | | | | | | | |
|---|---|---|---|---|---|---|---|---|
| 1 | Ⓐ Ⓑ Ⓒ Ⓓ | 15 | Ⓐ Ⓑ Ⓒ Ⓓ | 29 | Ⓐ Ⓑ Ⓒ Ⓓ |
| 2 | Ⓐ Ⓑ Ⓒ Ⓓ | 16 | Ⓐ Ⓑ Ⓒ Ⓓ | 30 | Ⓐ Ⓑ Ⓒ Ⓓ |
| 3 | Ⓐ Ⓑ Ⓒ Ⓓ | 17 | Ⓐ Ⓑ Ⓒ Ⓓ | 31 | Ⓐ Ⓑ Ⓒ Ⓓ |
| 4 | Ⓐ Ⓑ Ⓒ Ⓓ | 18 | Ⓐ Ⓑ Ⓒ Ⓓ | 32 | Ⓐ Ⓑ Ⓒ Ⓓ |
| 5 | Ⓐ Ⓑ Ⓒ Ⓓ | 19 | Ⓐ Ⓑ Ⓒ Ⓓ | 33 | Ⓐ Ⓑ Ⓒ Ⓓ |
| 6 | Ⓐ Ⓑ Ⓒ Ⓓ | 20 | Ⓐ Ⓑ Ⓒ Ⓓ | 34 | Ⓐ Ⓑ Ⓒ Ⓓ |
| 7 | Ⓐ Ⓑ Ⓒ Ⓓ | 21 | Ⓐ Ⓑ Ⓒ Ⓓ | 35 | Ⓐ Ⓑ Ⓒ Ⓓ |
| 8 | Ⓐ Ⓑ Ⓒ Ⓓ | 22 | Ⓐ Ⓑ Ⓒ Ⓓ | 36 | Ⓐ Ⓑ Ⓒ Ⓓ |
| 9 | Ⓐ Ⓑ Ⓒ Ⓓ | 23 | Ⓐ Ⓑ Ⓒ Ⓓ | 37 | Ⓐ Ⓑ Ⓒ Ⓓ |
| 10 | Ⓐ Ⓑ Ⓒ Ⓓ | 24 | Ⓐ Ⓑ Ⓒ Ⓓ | 38 | Ⓐ Ⓑ Ⓒ Ⓓ |
| 11 | Ⓐ Ⓑ Ⓒ Ⓓ | 25 | Ⓐ Ⓑ Ⓒ Ⓓ | 39 | Ⓐ Ⓑ Ⓒ Ⓓ |
| 12 | Ⓐ Ⓑ Ⓒ Ⓓ | 26 | Ⓐ Ⓑ Ⓒ Ⓓ | 40 | Ⓐ Ⓑ Ⓒ Ⓓ |
| 13 | Ⓐ Ⓑ Ⓒ Ⓓ | 27 | Ⓐ Ⓑ Ⓒ Ⓓ | 41 | Ⓐ Ⓑ Ⓒ Ⓓ |
| 14 | Ⓐ Ⓑ Ⓒ Ⓓ | 28 | Ⓐ Ⓑ Ⓒ Ⓓ | 42 | Ⓐ Ⓑ Ⓒ Ⓓ |

# Answer Sheet - Essay

Write your response in blue or black pen.

STUDENT NAME  _____

| Write your essay topic here. |
| --- |
| _____ |
| _____ |
| _____ |

Write your response here.

_____

_____

_____

_____

_____

_____

_____

_____

_____

_____

_____

_____

_____

_____

_____

_____

_____

_____

_____

_____

_____

_____

_____

_____

_____

(Answer Sheet - Essay continued)

# ISEE

Independent School Entrance Exam

# Upper Level
# Verbal Reasoning

# Practice Test 2

*This page intentionally left blank.*

# Section 1
# Verbal Reasoning

This section is divided into two parts that contain two different types of questions. As soon as you have completed Part One, answer the questions in Part Two. You may write in your test booklet. For each answer you select, fill in the corresponding circle on your answer document.

## Part One — Synonyms

Each question in Part One consists of a word in capital letters followed by four answer choices. Select the one word that is most nearly the same in meaning as the word in capital letters.

SAMPLE QUESTION:                                    SAMPLE ANSWER:

   EXTEND:                                          Ⓐ●ⒸⒹ

   (A) avoid
   (B) lengthen
   (C) criticize
   (D) discover

## Part Two — Sentence Completion

Each question in Part Two is made up of a sentence with one or two blanks. One blank indicates that one word is missing. Two blanks indicate that two words are missing. Each sentence is followed by four answer choices. Select the one word or pair of words that best completes the meaning of the sentence as a whole.

SAMPLE QUESTIONS:                                   SAMPLE ANSWERS:

   Unlike her older brother, who always acted --------,     ●ⒷⒸⒹ
   Cheryl preferred to take her time.

   (A) quickly
   (B) carefully
   (C) stupidly
   (D) wisely

   Whitewater rafting is both ------- and dangerous: rapids    ⒶⒷⒸ●
   may provide thrills, but they also threaten a rafter's ------.

   (A) ancient...pride
   (B) understandable...judgment
   (C) informative...freedom
   (D) exciting...safety

STOP. Do not go on until told to do so.    STOP

Acadian Academics - Upper Level ISEE Test 2          59

# Part One — Synonyms

**Directions:** Select the word that is most nearly the same in meaning as the word in capital letters.

1. RELEVANT:

   (A) rational
   (B) inappropriate
   (C) captive
   (D) applicable

2. VERIFY:

   (A) expand
   (B) interpret
   (C) confirm
   (D) analyze

3. EXTRACT:

   (A) remove
   (B) rescue
   (C) devour
   (D) import

4. ADJACENT:

   (A) neighboring
   (B) extensive
   (C) bold
   (D) desirable

5. INTEGRAL:

   (A) virtuous
   (B) stable
   (C) essential
   (D) dedicated

6. CONSOLIDATE:

   (A) forbid
   (B) merge
   (C) exclude
   (D) assist

7. SUCCINCT:

   (A) short
   (B) revealing
   (C) acidic
   (D) obvious

8. DIPLOMATIC:

   (A) tactful
   (B) foreign
   (C) alert
   (D) invasive

9. VOLATILE:

   (A) purposeful
   (B) envious
   (C) peaceful
   (D) unpredictable

10. PSYCHE:

   (A) shock
   (B) mind
   (C) therapy
   (D) program

11. GARNISH:

   (A)   feed
   (B)   decorate
   (C)   pack
   (D)   borrow

12. HASTE:

   (A)   disgust
   (B)   cement
   (C)   speed
   (D)   restraint

13. REVELRY:

   (A)   uprising
   (B)   crowd
   (C)   celebration
   (D)   accident

14. CHIDE:

   (A)   ring
   (B)   scold
   (C)   conform
   (D)   inspect

15. DETER:

   (A)   conclude
   (B)   appraise
   (C)   plant
   (D)   discourage

16. CHARLATAN:

   (A)   relative
   (B)   fake
   (C)   supporter
   (D)   gadget

17. EMBLEM:

   (A)   scheme
   (B)   bandage
   (C)   symbol
   (D)   center

# Part Two — Sentence Completion

**Directions:** Select the word or word pair that best completes the sentence.

18. American economic history is in part the story of ------- individuals who created thriving businesses to address the needs of society.

    (A) entrepreneurial
    (B) forgotten
    (C) materialistic
    (D) preoccupied

19. Vasily Kandinsky's paintings often utilize ------- contrasting colors; a single work may contain orange, magenta, cerulean blue, and cadmium yellow.

    (A) opposing
    (B) scant
    (C) inappropriate
    (D) numerous

20. Despite his impressive accomplishments in politics, Mohatma Gandhi retained his ------- throughout his life.

    (A) acumen
    (B) humility
    (C) wisdom
    (D) spirit

21. When a particle of matter and a particle of anti-matter collide, they ------- each other; this mutual destruction releases considerable energy.

    (A) magnify
    (B) annihilate
    (C) resist
    (D) undermine

22. Tommy's mother ------- his computer privileges, forcing him to do without online games for the evening.

    (A) enhanced
    (B) contemplated
    (C) revoked
    (D) expressed

23. Fearing that his good name would be ------- by false accusations of misconduct, Mr. Benedict invited reporters to examine his financial records.

    (A) honored
    (B) sullied
    (C) irritated
    (D) sustained

24. It took an accountant nearly a week to
------- the errors in Ms. Allen's tax return
so that it could be properly submitted to the
government.

   (A) comprehend
   (B) rectify
   (C) refine
   (D) incorporate

25. Mariana never stopped talking, and
her parents grew tired of her -------
conversation.

   (A) sensible
   (B) productive
   (C) incessant
   (D) capacious

26. Despite warnings that construction of such
a large suspension bridge across a turbulent
waterway would not be -------, New York
City successfully completed the Brooklyn
Bridge in 1883.

   (A) profitable
   (B) feasible
   (C) impractical
   (D) memorable

27. Residents of Coca, Ecuador fear that recent
oil drilling will contaminate the otherwise
------- environment of the rain forest.

   (A) polluted
   (B) brittle
   (C) pristine
   (D) restful

28. It takes courage to ------- a high-paying but
unsatisfying career in favor of a low-paying
but ------- one.

   (A) abandon…fulfilling
   (B) reject…disagreeable
   (C) initiate…edifying
   (D) cancel…elusive

29. Because the team had not ------- in more
than ten games, the players' morale was
-------.

   (A) prevailed…sinking
   (B) triumphed…soaring
   (C) lost…flagging
   (D) surrendered…aching

30. A good public relations firm can put a
positive spin on a news story by -------
unflattering details and ------- favorable
ones.

   (A) highlighting…masking
   (B) distributing…allocating
   (C) revealing…emphasizing
   (D) downplaying…accentuating

31. Historian Paul Addison criticizes the Allies'
haphazard, loosely targeted bombings of
Dresden in 1945 as an ------- attack yielding
little ------- gain.

   (A) inevitable…moral
   (B) irresponsible…logical
   (C) important…civilian
   (D) indiscriminate…strategic

32. The conviction of Jeffrey Skilling, a former millionaire executive, demonstrated that even the ------- cannot commit fraud with -------.

    (A) affluent…impunity
    (B) elite…ease
    (C) prosperous…ingenuity
    (D) powerless…security

33. It would be ------- to draw conclusions about the effectiveness of fish oil in lowering cholesterol levels before ------- testing has been conducted.

    (A) unwise…needless
    (B) prudent…thorough
    (C) destabilizing…collaborative
    (D) premature…comprehensive

34. Like a painter who ------- colors to achieve the right hue, the composer Eric Korngold uses unique combinations of instruments to create distinctive -------.

    (A) blends…timbres
    (B) separates…melodies
    (C) lightens…amenities
    (D) mingles…aspects

35. The effectiveness of short but demanding workouts in combating obesity shows that it is not the ------- of exercise that matters but rather its -------.

    (A) frequency…motivation
    (B) applicability…excitement
    (C) duration…intensity
    (D) objective…implementation

STOP. Do not go on until told to do so.  **STOP**

# ISEE
Independent School Entrance Exam

# Upper Level
# Quantitative Reasoning

# Practice Test 2

# Section 2
# Quantitative Reasoning

| 32 Questions | | Time: 30 minutes |
|---|---|---|

This section has two parts that contain two different kinds of questions. Do not pause after Part One. Continue working through Part Two. You may write in your test booklet.

Letters such as $x$ and $y$ stand for real numbers. All figures are drawn to scale unless otherwise stated.

**Part One — Word Problems**

Each question in Part One consists of a word problem followed by four answer choices. Select the best answer from the four choices given and fill in the corresponding circle on your answer document.

---

EXAMPLE 1:                                                    SAMPLE ANSWER

　　　　　　　　　　　　　　　　　　　　　　　　　　Ⓐ Ⓑ Ⓒ ●

Which of the following fractions is greater than $\frac{3}{4}$?

(A) $\frac{1}{5}$

(B) $\frac{1}{4}$

(C) $\frac{2}{5}$

(D) $\frac{4}{5}$

The correct answer is $\frac{4}{5}$, so circle D is darkened.

---

*Go on to the next page.* ➡

# QR

**Part Two — Quantitative Comparisons**

In Part Two, use the given information to compare the quantities given in Column A and Column B. Choose one of these four answer choices:

      (A)  The quantity in Column A is greater.

      (B)  The quantity in Column B is greater.

      (C)  The two quantities are equal.

      (D)  The relationship cannot be determined from the information given.

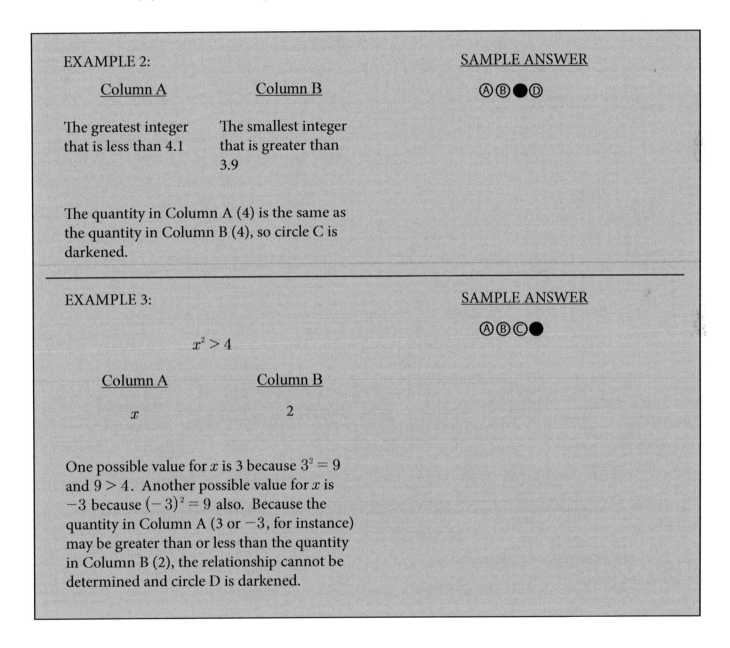

**EXAMPLE 2:**

<u>Column A</u>        <u>Column B</u>

The greatest integer that is less than 4.1    The smallest integer that is greater than 3.9

The quantity in Column A (4) is the same as the quantity in Column B (4), so circle C is darkened.

**SAMPLE ANSWER**

Ⓐ Ⓑ ● Ⓓ

**EXAMPLE 3:**

$$x^2 > 4$$

<u>Column A</u>        <u>Column B</u>

$x$          2

One possible value for $x$ is 3 because $3^2 = 9$ and $9 > 4$. Another possible value for $x$ is $-3$ because $(-3)^2 = 9$ also. Because the quantity in Column A (3 or $-3$, for instance) may be greater than or less than the quantity in Column B (2), the relationship cannot be determined and circle D is darkened.

**SAMPLE ANSWER**

Ⓐ Ⓑ Ⓒ ●

STOP. Do not go on until told to do so. **STOP**

## Part One — Word Problems

**Directions:** Choose the best answer from the four choices given.

1. If $y = 2x + 3$ and $-3 < x < 7$, which of the following expresses the range of possible values for y?

    (A) $-3 < y < 17$
    (B) $y < -3$ or $y > 17$
    (C) $y < 17$
    (D) $y > 3$

**Flowers in an Arrangement**

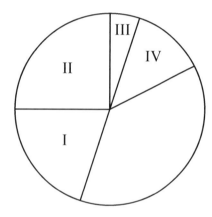

2. The circle graph above represents the proportion of different types of flowers in an arrangement of 40 flowers. 8 of the flowers are violets, 15 are daisies, 10 are roses, and the remainder are lilies and tulips. If there are more lilies than tulips, which section of the graph could represent the lilies?

    (A) Section I
    (B) Section II
    (C) Section III
    (D) Section IV

3. A car is traveling along a highway at 50 miles per hour. The driver sees traffic ahead and brakes, slowing to a rate of 25 miles per hour. He then continues driving. Which of the following graphs best represents the distance that the car travels during the time described?

    (A)
    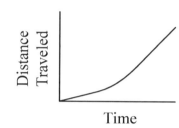

    (B)
    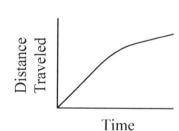

    (C)
    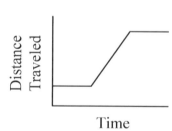

    (D)
    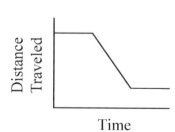

4.  If $\frac{x}{2} = \frac{7}{y}$, which expression is equal to $y$?

    (A)  $\frac{x}{14}$

    (B)  $\frac{7x}{2}$

    (C)  $\frac{7}{2x}$

    (D)  $\frac{14}{x}$

5.  A map of Greenville is drawn to scale so that 2 centimeters on the map represents 2.5 miles. If the distance between points A and B in Greenville is 12.5 miles, what is the distance between points A and B on the map?

    (A)  5 centimeters
    (B)  8 centimeters
    (C)  10 centimeters
    (D)  12 centimeters

6.  The graph shows Peter's speed as a function of time while he ran from home to school. He left home at 8:00 am and arrived at school at 8:40 am.

    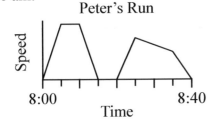

    Along the way, Peter stopped to rest. At what time did he start moving again?

    (A)  8:05
    (B)  8:10
    (C)  8:15
    (D)  8:20

7.  Tony and Doug are twin brothers who are in the same class of 10 students. They have no siblings besides each other. They ask each student in their class how many siblings he or she has and they make a bar chart of the results. If Tony and Doug include themselves in the data, which of the following bar charts could NOT be correct?

    (A)
    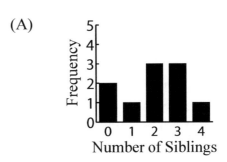

    (B)
    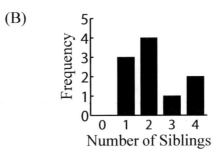

    (C)
    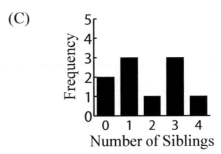

    (D)
    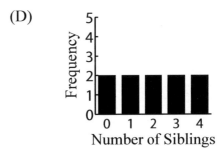

8. At a track meet, Mark competes in the long jump. The mean distance of his first two jumps is 92 inches. If the mean distance of all three of his jumps is 98 inches, what is the distance of his third jump?

(A) 95 inches

(B) 104 inches

(C) 106 inches

(D) 110 inches

9. A water tank that holds 10,000 gallons is half full. Water begins flowing into the tank from a hose at $x$ gallons per minute. At the same time, water begins leaking out of the tank at $y$ gallons per minute, where $x > y$. Which one piece of additional information, in gallons per hour, would be needed to determine how many hours it takes to fill the tank?

(A) $x$

(B) $y$

(C) The sum of $x$ and $y$

(D) The difference between $x$ and $y$

10. For any positive integer $n$, let $n!$ be the product of all integers from 1 to $n$, inclusive. What is the value of the expression below?

$$\frac{9!}{7!}$$

(A) 504

(B) 72

(C) 63

(D) $\frac{3}{2}$

11. What is the value of the following expression?

$$\frac{150 \times 5^2}{5 \times (5 + 5^2)}$$

(A) 1

(B) 5

(C) 25

(D) 125

12. The product of 3 different positive integers is 80. What is the greatest possible sum of the integers?

(A) 16

(B) 25

(C) 43

(D) 82

13. The weights of 8 students on a wrestling team are measured in pounds, and the following statistical measures are calculated for the weights:

| Mean | 150 |
| --- | --- |
| Median | 140 |
| Mode | 140 |
| Range | 32 |

Exactly two students on the team weigh 140 pounds. If 4 more students join the team, and each weighs more than 145 pounds, which of the statistical measures above must change?

(A) median

(B) range

(C) mode

(D) mean

14. In the figure, triangle ABC is similar to triangle DEF.

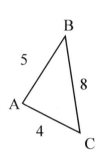 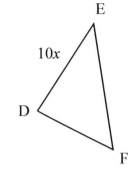

What is the perimeter of triangle DEF?

(A)  $17x$
(B)  $34x$
(C)  $10x + 12$
(D)  $10x + 24$

15. Let $a \oplus b = 2a - b$. What is the value of $3 \oplus (5 \oplus 1)$ ?

(A)  $-3$
(B)  $0$
(C)  $1$
(D)  $15$

16. If $4(a+b)^2 = 4a^2 + kab + 4b^2$, what is the value of $k$?

(A)  16
(B)  8
(C)  4
(D)  2

17. If $z$ is a prime number, which of the following represents the least common multiple of $2z^2$ and $6z$?

(A)  $12z^3$
(B)  $12z^2$
(C)  $6z^2$
(D)  $3z$

18. The object below consists of six cubes joined at their faces. One of the cubes is completely hidden.

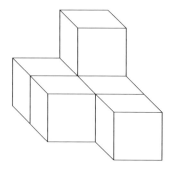

Which of the following is a pair of objects that could be combined to form the object above?

(A)

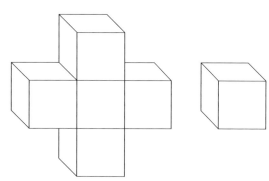

(B)

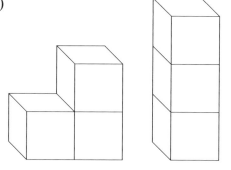

(C)

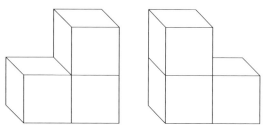

(D)

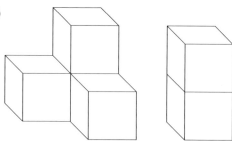

**Part Two—Quantitative Comparisons**

**Directions:** Using the information given in each question, compare the quantity in Column A to the quantity in Column B. All questions in Part Two have these answer choices:

(A)    The quantity in Column A is greater.
(B)    The quantity in Column B is greater.
(C)    The two quantities are equal.
(D)    The relationship cannot be determined from the information given.

---

Triangle X

Rectangle Y

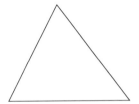 

Note: Figures not drawn to scale

The perimeter of Triangle X is 18 centimeters. The perimeter of Rectangle Y is 16 centimeters.

| Column A | Column B |
|---|---|
| 19. The area of Triangle X | The area of Rectangle Y |

---

| Column A | Column B |
|---|---|
| 20.    $pq(p-1)$ | $pq(p-q)$ |

---

Marshaun makes a list of 10 consecutive even integers, starting at 6.

| Column A | Column B |
|---|---|
| 21. The last integer in the list | 24 |

---

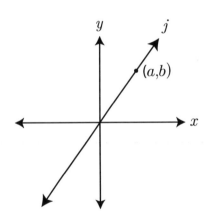

Line $j$ passes through the point $(a,b)$ as shown above, where $b > a$.

| Column A | Column B |
|---|---|
| 22.    1 | The slope of line $j$ |

---

---

**Answer choices for all questions on this page:**

(A) The quantity in Column A is greater.
(B) The quantity in Column B is greater.
(C) The two quantities are equal.
(D) The relationship cannot be determined from the information given.

---

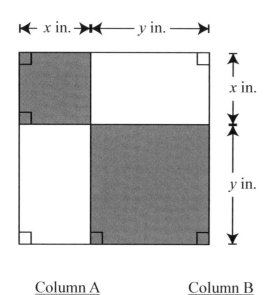

|  | Column A | Column B |
|---|---|---|
| 23. | The shaded area | $x^2 + y^2$ inches$^2$ |

---

The perimeter of a rectangle is $p$ inches.

|  | Column A | Column B |
|---|---|---|
| 24. | The largest possible area of the rectangle | $\dfrac{p^2}{16}$ inches$^2$ |

|  | Column A | Column B |
|---|---|---|
| 25. | $3(4 + x) + 3x$ | $3 \times 4 + 3(2x + 1)$ |

---

A bag contains only pennies and nickels. A coin is selected randomly from the bag, then a second coin is selected from the bag without replacing the first.

|  | Column A | Column B |
|---|---|---|
| 26. | The probability that both coins are pennies | The probability that both coins are nickels |

---

Parker, Vanessa and Seth all live on the same straight road. Vanessa's house is 3.2 miles from Parker's house and Seth's house is 4.9 miles from Vanessa's house.

|  | Column A | Column B |
|---|---|---|
| 27. | The distance from Seth's house to Parker's house | 8.1 miles |

$$x < 0$$

| | Column A | Column B |
|---|---|---|
| 28. | $\sqrt{x^2}$ | $x$ |

| | Column A | Column B |
|---|---|---|
| 29. | $(9.7)^4$ | $\dfrac{(97)^4}{10,000}$ |

In a math class, one student is chosen randomly to answer a question. There are 12 girls and 8 boys in the class. If a girl is chosen, the probability that she knows the answer is $\frac{2}{3}$. If a boy is chosen, the probability that he knows the answer is $\frac{1}{2}$.

| | Column A | Column B |
|---|---|---|
| 30. | The number of students in the class who know the answer | 12 |

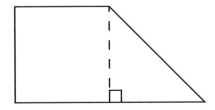

The figure shown is composed of a square and an isosceles right triangle. The area of the triangle is 18 square inches.

| | Column A | Column B |
|---|---|---|
| 31. | 24 inches | The perimeter of the figure |

Jim's Hardware Store purchases hammers for $16 each. The store then offers to sell the hammers for a list price of $24 apiece. Because none sell, the store then offers the hammers for a discount price of 25% off the list price.

| | Column A | Column B |
|---|---|---|
| 32. | The profit the store makes per hammer sold at the discount price | $4 |

*This page intentionally left blank.*

# ISEE
Independent School Entrance Exam

# Upper Level
# Reading Comprehension

# Practice Test 2

*This page intentionally left blank.*

# Section 3
# Reading Comprehension

**30 Questions**

**Time: 30 minutes**

This section contains five short reading passages. Each passage is followed by six questions based on its content. Answer the questions following each passage on the basis of what is stated or implied in that passage. You may write in your test booklet.

STOP. Do not go on
until told to do so.

**STOP**

Questions 1–6

1     For nearly all of us, the first teacher is
2 family. Family teaches us to walk and talk,
3 to eat with utensils, and to hold hands when
4 crossing the street. Our parents teach us about
5 our family histories: they introduce us to
6 grandparents, aunts, uncles, and cousins. They
7 teach us about culture, exposing us to traditions
8 that define our respective ways of life. From
9 our siblings we learn not only how to share
10 and to play, but also how to argue and to make
11 peace.
12     This period of familial learning passes
13 quickly, though. In the United States, children
14 soon glide into the hands of professional
15 educators, often by the age of four or five. They
16 transition from learning about relatives and
17 ancestors to studying Christopher Columbus and
18 George Washington and the other strangers of
19 history. The means of learning change as well,
20 as books (also written by strangers) become the
21 primary source of knowledge.
22     In West Africa, the transition happens
23 differently. While children do attend school,
24 society places a greater emphasis on the local
25 community and its recent past. Cultural

26 knowledge is passed down in songs and stories
27 rather than in writing. This oral history is
28 preserved by people known as griots, who spend
29 their lives accumulating local lore and rituals.
30     Griots are many things to their communities.
31 They are historians, poets, and master
32 storytellers and singers. The know the precise
33 genealogy of local families generations back
34 and recite legends exactly as they have been
35 told for hundreds of years. But they are also
36 improvisational artists, incorporating current
37 events, audience reactions, and their immediate
38 surroundings into a performance. Perhaps this
39 is a holdover from the days when griots were
40 also royal advisors, applying the lessons of
41 generations past to a current crisis.
42     Not just anyone can be a griot. In keeping
43 with the emphasis on family in West African
44 culture, the profession is passed down from
45 parents to their children. Griots often marry
46 other griots, and their children are immersed in
47 the world of ritual and tradition their parents
48 inhabit. Many of those children also grow up to
49 be griots, adding another story of family to the
50 local canon.

1. In lines 18-19, the phrase "strangers of history" refers to

   (A) history teachers a child doesn't know
   (B) historical figures unrelated to a child
   (C) people a child has met, then forgotten
   (D) a child's ancestors who have died

2. The author would most likely agree with which statement?

   (A) Family is less important in the United States than in West Africa
   (B) Oral history is superior to written history
   (C) Ways of preserving knowledge vary from culture to culture
   (D) Children should learn from relatives, not from strangers

3. The passage states that children learn about all of the following from family EXCEPT

   (A) their ancestors
   (B) resolving disputes
   (C) safety precautions
   (D) reading books

4. The passage suggests that, in the past, a griot might have had to improvise because he

   (A) needed to provide guidance
   (B) couldn't hold his audience's attention
   (C) had forgotten the details of a story
   (D) felt constrained by the strict rules of his profession

5. According to the last paragraph (lines 42-50), the griot's profession is

   (A) difficult and time-consuming
   (B) ritualistic and boring
   (C) open to anyone with West African family
   (D) limited to direct descendants of griots

6. As used in line 29, the word "lore" most nearly means

   (A) objects
   (B) ceremonies
   (C) tales
   (D) families

Questions 7–12

1     The world of literature is filled with
2 novelists of prodigious output: writers who
3 published a great number of books over
4 the course of their careers.  More rare (and
5 fascinating), however, are those authors who
6 achieved critical acclaim with a single book—
7 and who never went on to write another one.
8     In 1834, a 14-year-old girl named Anna
9 Sewell slipped while walking home from
10 school and injured her ankles so badly that she
11 was disabled for the rest of her life.  She made
12 frequent use of horse-drawn carriages to get
13 around and developed a deep love for horses
14 and concern for their well-being.  Throughout
15 her life Anna performed many charitable
16 works, edited children's books, and mingled
17 with writers, artists, and philosophers.  In
18 1871 her health declined, and for the next six
19 years she penned a novel while bedridden.
20 *Black Beauty,* narrated from the perspective
21 of its title character, a horse, proved an instant
22 success on its publication in 1877.  Sewell
23 passed away six months after its initial release,
24 living long enough to see her book achieve its
25 goal of inducing "kindness, sympathy, and an
26 understanding treatment of horses."
27     Harper Lee's classic *To Kill a Mockingbird*
28 received  the Pulitzer Prize for Fiction in 1961,
29 was voted "Best Novel of the Century" by
30 the Library Journal in 1999, and earned Lee
31 the Presidential Medal of Freedom for her
32 contribution to literature.  Yet Lee never went
33 on to write another book.  *To Kill a Mockingbird*
34 draws on observations and experiences from

35 her childhood in Monroeville, Alabama, and
36 deals with issues of race, class, gender roles,
37 and social justice.   It was an instant success
38 upon its publication in 1960, but Lee found the
39 sudden attention overwhelming.  Later in her
40 life, Lee relayed through a close friend why she
41 had chosen not to write another novel: "Two
42 reasons: one, I wouldn't go through the pressure
43 and publicity I went through with *To Kill a*
44 *Mockingbird* for any amount of money. Second,
45 I have said what I wanted to say and I will not
46 say it again."
47     Holden Caulfield, the protagonist of J.D.
48 Salinger's *The Catcher in the Rye*, has become
49 an icon for adolescent alienation, defiance,
50 and rebellion.  The novel itself has sold more
51 than 65 million copies, in almost all of the
52 world's major languages, and was named by
53 Modern Library as one of the hundred best
54 English-language novels of the 20th century.
55 Since its publication in 1951, it has sparked
56 controversy as well as critical acclaim with
57 its liberal use of profanity and mature themes,
58 yet it remains one of the best-loved and
59 most-taught books in the United States.  J.D.
60 Salinger, however, later became as famous for
61 his notorious reclusiveness as for his book.  He
62 never published another novel after *Catcher*,
63 and conducted his last interview in 1980.  In
64 1974, he told The New York Times: "There is
65 a marvelous peace in not publishing ... I like to
66 write. I love to write. But I write just for myself
67 and my own pleasure."

7. The author seems to be most interested in

    (A) what makes one novel better than others

    (B) how writers are able to produce so many books

    (C) the reclusive habits of some writers

    (D) why some writers don't publish much

8. The quotations from Harper Lee and J.D. Salinger suggest that both authors

    (A) have stopped writing entirely

    (B) dislike the publishing process

    (C) have nothing further to say

    (D) no longer need to make money

9. Anna Sewell's love of horses was an indirect result of

    (A) an accident early in her life

    (B) conversations with well-educated people

    (C) her declining health in middle age

    (D) the search for a good book topic

10. In line 2, the word "prodigious" most nearly means

    (A) wasteful

    (B) enormous

    (C) talented

    (D) uneven

11. The passage answers all of the following questions EXCEPT

    (A) Who is the main character of *A Catcher in the Rye*?

    (B) What themes does *To Kill a Mockingbird* address?

    (C) Did Anna Sewell receive any literary awards?

    (D) Where did Harper Lee grow up?

12. Compared with J.D. Salinger, Anna Sewell is described as more

    (A) sociable

    (B) controversial

    (C) well-mannered

    (D) loving

Questions 13–18

1  When Jeremy and I finished with baseball
2  practice on Friday afternoons, we would stop
3  by the general store and relax at the rarely used
4  pool table in the side room. I always used the
5  long cue stick with a shallow taper, good for
6  striking balls far from the edge of the table but
7  hard to balance; he used the shorter cue that
8  offered more predictable control but less reach.
9  This was a reflection of ourselves as much as
10  our preferences in pool: I, the ambitious striver,
11  over-extended and constantly expanding my
12  horizons; and Jeremy, the devoted homebody
13  with little interest in what lay beyond his ken.
14  One such afternoon in May, I stood studying
15  the table. Jeremy was, not surprisingly, winning
16  by a good margin. I had made the same
17  mistakes I always did, sacrificing the current
18  shot in favor of planning for the next one.
19  Jeremy had methodically knocked his balls into
20  the pockets one at a time, and now he had only
21  two remaining. I had six.
22  "Doesn't look good for you," Jeremy said
23  with a grin. "That's ok. I beat you at pool. You
24  beat me at everything else—except maybe
25  skipping rocks. Maybe all of that overhand
26  pitching has messed up your form. No sidearm
27  left in you. We'll see when we go camping out
28  on Red Island this summer."
29  There was a silence between us then for
30  several long seconds. I looked down. The
31  ceiling fan overhead creaked softly. Jeremy
32  stood across the table, awaiting my clever reply
33  to his calculated thrust. I couldn't join in his
34  good-natured ribbing though. I had news. "I
35  can't go to Red Island again this summer. I've
36  been accepted to the program at Woodbridge.
37  I'll be there from late June through August."
38  There was another silence. "I didn't know
39  that," Jeremy said quietly.
40  I looked at him then, just catching a glimpse
41  of his crestfallen look before it turned cool and
42  hard. He bit his lip, turned his back and rapped
43  his knuckles forcefully on the edge of the
44  table, a signal to take my turn but also maybe
45  something more pointed. I picked up the cue
46  and leaned forward to shoot, wondering what I
47  had sacrificed in order to expand my horizons
48  that summer.

13. The "calculated thrust" the narrator mentions in line 33 refers to

    (A) a specific technique for skipping rocks
    (B) a targeted insult related to baseball
    (C) a well-planned shot with the cue stick
    (D) the most efficient form for pitching a baseball

14. The passage mainly serves to

    (A) outline the qualities that make a good pool player
    (B) point out that silence can be more meaningful than words
    (C) characterize two people and a tension between them
    (D) illustrate how a friendship can be broken

15. In the first paragraph, what purpose does the author's description of different cue sticks serve?

    (A) It helps to explain why Jeremy usually beats the narrator at pool.
    (B) It suggests that Jeremy is more adventuresome than the narrator.
    (C) It foreshadows an event in the narrator's future.
    (D) It provides a metaphor for differences between the narrator and Jeremy.

16. In line 13, the word "ken" most nearly means

    (A) immediate family
    (B) realm of experience
    (C) athletic abilities
    (D) unimaginative thinking

17. In line 45, the author uses the word "cue" as

    (A) a pun, because it has two possible meanings in this context
    (B) an oxymoron, because it means the opposite of the word "signal"
    (C) an allusion, because it refers indirectly to a famous work of art
    (D) a cliché, because it has already been used several times in the passage

18. It can be inferred from the second paragraph (lines 14-21) that the narrator

    (A) always loses to Jeremy in pool
    (B) is not methodical in his approach to pool
    (C) cannot knock any balls into the pockets
    (D) uses similar strategies each time he plays pool

Questions 19–24

1    You see the signs everywhere. Deli counters
2 advertise meat with slogans like "our assault
3 on salt continues." Banners on the subway
4 encourage riders to "Compare labels. Choose
5 less sodium." The doctor's office has a nice
6 new dietary pamphlet with a circle graph
7 showing a miniature sliver for "salt."
8    Given all of the attention that sodium (a
9 component of salt) gets in the world of public
10 health, it would seem that excessive salt is as
11 unhealthy for us as smoking or alcoholism. The
12 first anti-salt messages appeared in 1972, when
13 the National High Blood Pressure Education
14 Program included warnings about the dangers
15 of salt in its published materials. Since then,
16 the down-with-salt rallying cry has spread like
17 wildfire through public and non-profit heath
18 organizations, including the U.S. Department of
19 Agriculture and the American Heart Association.
20 Critics of excessive salt consumption cite a
21 2005 report by the prestigious Institute of
22 Medicine, which recommended sodium intake
23 levels between only 1,500 and 2,300 milligrams
24 per day. Some groups have lobbied the federal
25 government to regulate the salt content of
26 processed foods, from which many Americans
27 get the majority of their daily sodium.
28    Despite four decades of salt hysteria,
29 the scientific justification for limited salt
30 consumption is surprisingly thin. Much of
31 it, in fact, is based on a single study in which
32 participants were assigned to eat high, medium,
33 or low-sodium diets for 30 days. Researchers

34 observed that lower sodium intake corresponded
35 with decreased blood pressure. Since high
36 blood pressure is associated with heart disease
37 and strokes, it appeared that a low-sodium diet
38 could help prevent serious illness.
39    This reasoning seems entirely plausible on
40 the surface. However, subsequent studies of
41 the direct relationship between salt intake and
42 negative outcomes like heart attack, stroke, and
43 death revealed a very different picture. Most
44 such studies found no appreciable benefit to
45 following a very low-sodium diet. In fact, in
46 certain circumstances, low salt intake seemed to
47 actually increase the risk of death.
48    So why all the alarm about sodium? At least
49 part of the answer must lie in a phenomenon
50 called confirmation bias. When presented with
51 evidence for or against a hypothesis, people
52 tend to favor the evidence that confirms their
53 prior beliefs. The anti-salt message has been so
54 strong for so long that many researchers may
55 suffer from such bias.
56    Thankfully, some research is finally cutting
57 through the haze of preconceived notions. The
58 Institute of Medicine recently issued a follow-
59 up to its 2005 report. This new assessment
60 proclaims that the evidence against salt is
61 "inconsistent and insufficient" and consequently
62 "does not support recommendations to lower
63 sodium intake." It is time that other institutions
64 like the American Heart Association (which
65 maintains its strong anti-salt stance) consider
66 revising their positions as well.

19. The overall tone of the passage can best be described as

(A) detached and nonpartisan
(B) impassive and indifferent
(C) strong and argumentative
(D) ambiguous and indecisive

20. Which of the following characterizes the structure of the fourth paragraph (lines 39-47)? The author

(A) acknowledges a point, then offers a rebuttal
(B) states a thesis, then gives supporting evidence
(C) rejects an idea, then gives reasons for that rejection
(D) affirms one perspective, then considers others

21. According to the passage, confirmation bias is a result of

(A) low salt intake
(B) weak evidence
(C) untested hypotheses
(D) preconceived notions

22. The passage indicates that which of the following organizations has changed its position on salt intake?

(A) The Institute of Medicine
(B) The U.S. Department of Agriculture
(C) The American Heart Association
(D) The National High Blood Pressure Education Program

23. In line 44, the word "appreciable" most nearly means

(A) likeable
(B) valuable
(C) detectable
(D) understandable

24. The passage is best summarized by which of the following statements?

(A) Large amounts of salt are bad for one's health.
(B) The dangers of salt are overstated.
(C) High blood pressure causes heart disease.
(D) Many authorities recommend a low-salt diet.

Questions 25–30

1     When Jerome Robbins—a legendary
2 American choreographer, producer, and
3 director—passed away in 1998, only one
4 small photograph stood at his bedside: that
5 of a beautiful middle-aged woman with
6 laughing eyes. The woman was Tanaquil
7 LeClercq, former principal dancer with
8 George Balanchine's New York City Ballet,
9 Balanchine's fifth wife, and Robbins's lifelong
10 friend and muse. Yet Robbins was only one of
11 many that LeClercq inspired throughout her
12 storied career.
13     Born in Paris in 1929 to a French intellectual
14 and his American bride, LeClercq grew up in
15 New York among the city's artistic elite. In
16 1941, at age 12, she entered the prestigious
17 School of American Ballet, and at 15,
18 Balanchine cast her in a piece commissioned
19 for a polio benefit. In it, Balanchine played
20 the spectre of Polio, and LeClercq played his
21 victim, struck down and paralyzed. The casting
22 would later prove to be an unsettling omen.
23     LeClercq went on to become the darling
24 of the New York City Ballet; she captured the
25 hearts of the public, the critics—and Balanchine

26 himself, who married her on New Year's Eve
27 in 1952. Balanchine and Robbins, along with
28 Merce Cunningham and countless others,
29 created ballets for her. They marveled at her
30 astonishing versatility and charisma. Elegant,
31 cosmopolitan, witty, and chic, she was adored
32 by fans and critics, photographed by Vogue, and
33 immortalized in poet Frank O'Hara's *Ode to*
34 *Tanaquil LeClercq.*
35     Tragically, LeClercq was stricken with polio
36 and paralyzed from the waist down while on
37 tour in Europe in 1956. She was 27 years old.
38 She would never dance again. LeClercq's poise
39 and intelligence remained untouched, however,
40 and for the rest of her life she continued to
41 travel, socialize, run two households, and even
42 teach ballet, "using her hands and arms as
43 legs and feet," according to a former student.
44 Although she and Balanchine eventually
45 divorced, she remained close friends with
46 Jerome Robbins until the end of his life—and
47 remained a beloved figure in the world of ballet,
48 a world she had forever imprinted with her
49 unique style and grace.

25. The author's mention of the polio benefit (lines 19-22) is an example of

    (A) metaphor
    (B) onomatopoeia
    (C) foreshadowing
    (D) hyperbole

26. The author's overall attitude toward LeClercq is best described as

    (A) admiring
    (B) patronizing
    (C) cautious
    (D) ambivalent

27. In line 48, "imprinted" most nearly means

    (A) written
    (B) marked
    (C) recorded
    (D) tarnished

28. The author suggests that Balanchine, Robbins and Cunningham created ballets for LeClercq because she

    (A) was physically beautiful
    (B) worked well with other dancers
    (C) possessed superior intelligence
    (D) could do a variety of things well

29. The passage indicates that after 1956, LeClercq

    (A) continued to dance
    (B) struggled to find romance
    (C) felt imprisoned by her disease
    (D) adjusted to her limitations

30. LeClercq apparently had the most lasting relationship with whom?

    (A) George Balanchine
    (B) Jerome Robbins
    (C) Merce Cunningham
    (D) Frank O'Hara

STOP. If there is time, you may check your work on this section only.

STOP

*This page intentionally left blank.*

# ISEE

Independent School Entrance Exam

# Upper Level
# Mathematics Achievement

# Practice Test 2

*This page intentionally left blank.*

# MA

## Section 4
## Mathematics Achievement

Choose the best answer from the four choices given.  Fill in the corresponding circle on your answer document.  You may write in the test booklet.

SAMPLE QUESTION:

SAMPLE ANSWER

Ⓐ●ⒸⒹ

What number is 40% of 50?

(A)  10
(B)  20
(C)  30
(D)  40

The correct answer is 20, so circle B is darkened.

1. What is the value of the expression $4.01 \times 10^6 + 3.24 \times 10^3$?

    (A) $7.25 \times 10^3$
    (B) $4.334 \times 10^4$
    (C) $4.0424 \times 10^5$
    (D) $4.01324 \times 10^6$

2. Which expression is equivalent to the expression $\dfrac{m^2}{4} - \dfrac{n - m^2}{8}$?

    (A) $\dfrac{m^2 - n}{8}$
    (B) $\dfrac{3m^2 - n}{8}$
    (C) $\dfrac{n}{4}$
    (D) $\dfrac{2m^2 - n}{-4}$

3. A circle has a center of $(3, 1)$ and a radius of 4 grid units. Which of the following could NOT be a point on the circle?

    (A) $(7, 1)$
    (B) $(-1, 1)$
    (C) $(3, -3)$
    (D) $(3, 4)$

4. At a beach, a vendor sells ten ice cream cones. Eight contain chocolate ice cream and two contain vanilla ice cream. The price of a vanilla cone is twice the price of a chocolate cone. If the mean price of all ten cones, chocolate and vanilla, is $3.60, what is the price of a chocolate cone?

    (A) $1.80
    (B) $2.00
    (C) $3.00
    (D) $3.60

5. Which gives all values of $x$ for which $|2x + 1| - 4 = 0$?

    (A) $x = \dfrac{3}{2}$
    (B) $x = \dfrac{3}{2}$ or $x = -\dfrac{5}{2}$
    (C) $x = -\dfrac{3}{2}$ or $x = \dfrac{5}{2}$
    (D) $x = -\dfrac{3}{2}$ or $x = -\dfrac{5}{2}$

6. Which value is NOT equal to $\dfrac{5}{4}$?

    (A) $1 + .25$
    (B) $\dfrac{10}{8}$
    (C) $2 \times (.625)$
    (D) $\dfrac{25}{16}$

7. Carter has 7 colors of paint. He will select 2 of these colors to use in a painting. How many combinations of 2 colors are possible from the 7 colors available?

   (A) 21
   (B) 42
   (C) 49
   (D) 128

8. If $a(2+3)+1 = 2(a+1)+3$, what is the value of $a$?

   (A) $-1$

   (B) 1

   (C) $\frac{4}{3}$

   (D) the equation is true for all values of $a$

9. 320,570 is equal to which of the following?

   (A) $320 \times 1,000 + 5 \times 100 + 7 \times 10$
   (B) $320 \times 1,000 + 500 \times 100 + 7 \times 10$
   (C) $32 \times 1,000 + 5 \times 100 + 7 \times 10$
   (D) $32 \times 1,000 + 5 \times 100 + 7$

10. The graph below shows the number of movies seen in the past month by students in Kevin's class. The numbers on the horizontal axis represent the number of movies seen, and the numbers on the vertical axis represent the percentage of students in Kevin's class who saw that number of movies.

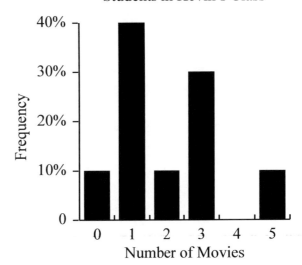

Number of Movies Seen by Students in Kevin's Class

If there are 30 students in Kevin's class, how many students saw the mean number of movies?

   (A) 3
   (B) 9
   (C) 12
   (D) None - the mean number of movies is not a whole number

11. A company would like to know how satisfied its employees are with their jobs, so it conducts a survey. Which sample would give the most trustworthy data about employees in the company?

(A) A random sample of executives at a meeting
(B) A random sample of employees in the sales department
(C) A random sample from a list of all employees
(D) Employees who chose to respond to an email asking for feedback

12. Which of the following is equal to $(2 - .25)^3$?

(A) $\dfrac{7^3}{2^3}$

(B) $\dfrac{(5 + 2)^3}{4^3}$

(C) $2^3 - .25^3$

(D) $(2 - .25)(2^2 - .25^2)$

13. Which of the following statements is NOT true?

(A) $\pi$ is an irrational number
(B) $\sqrt{7}$ is a real number
(C) $-\sqrt{11}$ is an imaginary number
(D) $\sqrt{-4}$ is an imaginary number

14. A lifeguard at a pool recorded the number of swimmers who needed assistance every day for 15 days. The table below summarizes his data.

| Number of swimmers who needed assistance | Number of days on which that number of swimmers needed assistance |
|---|---|
| 0 | 2 |
| 1 | 0 |
| 2 | 3 |
| 3 | 2 |
| 4 | 2 |
| 5 | 1 |
| 6 | 5 |

What is the median number of swimmers who needed assistance?

(A) 2
(B) 3
(C) 4
(D) 5

15. For what values of $x$ is it true that $\dfrac{1 + x^2}{(x + 1)(x + 2)} = 0$?

(A) $x = -1$ only
(B) $x = -1$ and $x = 1$
(C) $x = -2$ and $x = -1$ and $x = 1$
(D) There are no real values of $x$ for which the equation is true.

16. Which graph represents the solution set of the disjunction $2x < -8$ or $x - 1 > 2$?

(A)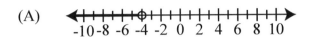
-10 -8 -6 -4 -2 0 2 4 6 8 10

(B)
-10 -8 -6 -4 -2 0 2 4 6 8 10

(C)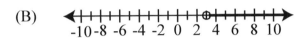
-10 -8 -6 -4 -2 0 2 4 6 8 10

(D)
-10 -8 -6 -4 -2 0 2 4 6 8 10

17. If $a$ is a positive number, which expression is equivalent to $a^4 \sqrt{10}$?

(A) $10\sqrt{a^2}$
(B) $\sqrt{10a^2}$
(C) $\sqrt{10a^4}$
(D) $\sqrt{10a^8}$

18. A printer can print 12 pages in one minute. A booklet contains 30 pages. Which expression is equal to the number of booklets the printer can print in one hour?

(A) $\dfrac{12 \times 30}{60}$

(B) $\dfrac{12 \times 60}{30}$

(C) $\dfrac{12}{30 \times 60}$

(D) $\dfrac{60 \times 30}{12}$

19. Sebastian throws a dart at the circular game board below, which is divided into wedges of equal size.

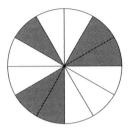

Sebastian earns 24 points if the dart lands in a shaded wedge and 0 points if the dart lands in an unshaded wedge. Assuming the dart is equally likely to land on any point on the board, what is the expected number of points Sebastian earns by throwing one dart?

(A) 24
(B) 10
(C) 8
(D) 2

20. In the figure below, AB = BC.

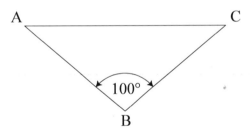

What is the measure of $\angle$BAC?

(A) 50°
(B) 45°
(C) 40°
(D) 35°

21. Trevor earns $60 per day selling t-shirts, plus $3 for each t-shirt that he sells. Which of the following is an amount that Trevor could NOT earn in a day selling t-shirts?

    (A) $60
    (B) $81
    (C) $100
    (D) $108

22. If $t$ and $s$ are prime numbers, which of the following is a common multiple of $6s^2t^3$ and $9st^5$?

    (A) $18s^3t^5$
    (B) $18st^3$
    (C) $3s^3t^5$
    (D) $72s^2t^3$

23. A movie showing consists of four two-minute previews followed by one 97-minute feature. Django arrived late and missed $\frac{1}{5}$ of the showing. How many minutes of the feature did Django miss?

    (A) 21 minutes
    (B) 20 minutes
    (C) 13 minutes
    (D) 12 minutes

24. Which is the most reasonable unit for measuring the time between sunrise and sunset on a given day?

    (A) miles
    (B) hours
    (C) weeks
    (D) milliseconds

25. Fahrenheit temperature, $F$, is related to Celsius temperature, $C$, by the formula $F = \frac{9}{5}C + 32$. If the Celsius temperature last Saturday was 15°, what was the Fahrenheit temperature?

    (A) 41°
    (B) 59°
    (C) 64°
    (D) 77°

26. Fruit punch is made from orange juice and apple juice. The ratio of orange juice to apple juice is 3:2. If a carton of fruit punch contains 15 ounces of orange juice, how many ounces of fruit punch does the carton contain?

    (A) 25 ounces
    (B) 21 ounces
    (C) 20 ounces
    (D) 10 ounces

27. If the population of Oxford is 20% greater than the population of Riverside, which of the following statements is true?

    (A) The population of Riverside is 20% less than the population of Oxford
    (B) The population of Oxford is 120% of the population of Riverside
    (C) The population of Riverside is 80% of the population of Oxford
    (D) The population of Oxford is 125% of the population of Riverside

28. The height of a ball thrown straight upward is given by $h = -30t^2 + st$, where $h$ is the height of the ball in feet, $t$ is the number of seconds since the ball was thrown, and $s$ is the speed at which the ball was thrown (in feet per second). Two seconds after the ball was thrown, the ball has a height of 20 feet. At what speed was the ball thrown?

(A) 40 feet per second
(B) 70 feet per second
(C) 80 feet per second
(D) 140 feet per second

29. Which expression is equivalent to $b^2 - 4a^2$?

(A) $(b + 2a)(b - 2a)$
(B) $(b - 2a)(b - 2a)$
(C) $(b + 4a)(b - 4a)$
(D) $(b - 4a)(b - 4a)$

30. For how many real values of $x$ is it true that $x^3 = x$?

(A) 3
(B) 2
(C) 1
(D) 0

31. Marta weighed some books on a shelf in her school's library. The box-and-whisker plot below summarizes the weights of the books in pounds.

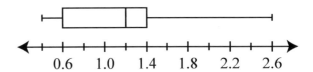

What is the difference between the median weight of the books and the weight of the heaviest book?

(A) 1.0 pounds
(B) 1.1 pounds
(C) 1.2 pounds
(D) 1.4 pounds

32. If $3\begin{bmatrix} y \\ 2 \end{bmatrix} = \begin{bmatrix} 27 \\ 6 \end{bmatrix}$, what is the value of $y$?

(A) 9
(B) 12
(C) 18
(D) 24

33. If $a = b$ and $x = y$, which of the following COULD be true?

(A) $a = x$ and $b \neq y$
(B) $a = x$ and $a \neq y$
(C) $a = x$ and $x \neq b$
(D) $a \neq x$ and $b \neq y$

34. Line $s$ is shown along with point $P$.

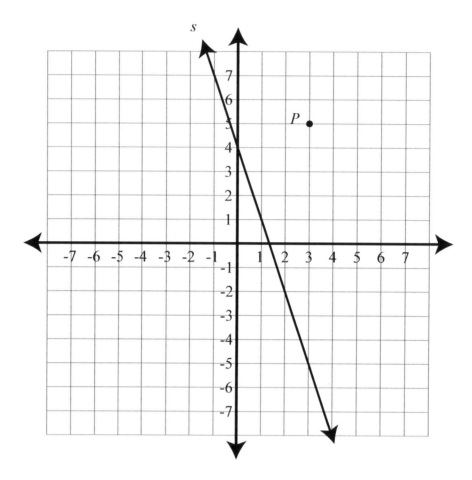

If point $P$ is on line $t$ (not shown), and line $t$ is perpendicular to line $s$, which of the following could be another point on line $t$?

(A) (6,6)

(B) (6,4)

(C) (4,2)

(D) (4,8)

35. A string is attached to the ground with a stake. The other end of the string is attached to a kite flying in the air, as shown in the figure.

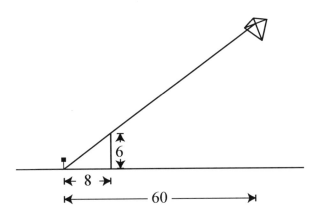

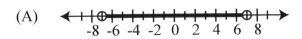

At a point 8 horizontal feet from the stake, the string is 6 feet above the ground. If the kite is flying above a point that is 60 horizontal feet from the stake, how high is the kite?

(A) 45 feet
(B) 58 feet
(C) 68 feet
(D) 80 feet

36. Which of the following graphs shows the solution set of $|x + 5| < 2$?

(A)

-8 -6 -4 -2 0 2 4 6 8

(B)

-8 -6 -4 -2 0 2 4 6 8

(C)

-8 -6 -4 -2 0 2 4 6 8

(D)

-8 -6 -4 -2 0 2 4 6 8

37. The bar graph below shows the number of cars sold at a car dealership for 8 different weeks.

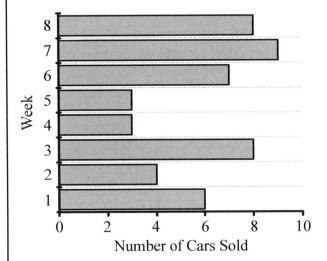

What is the median number of cars sold for the 8 weeks shown?

(A) 3
(B) 6.5
(C) 7.5
(D) 8

38. Which of the following numerical expressions represents a negative even integer?

(A) $3^2 - (-5)^2$
(B) $3^2 - 4^2$
(C) $-3^2 + (-5)^2$
(D) $-3^2 - 4^2$

39. The figure below shows a large parallelogram divided into 13 smaller, identical parallelograms and an irregularly shaped shaded region.

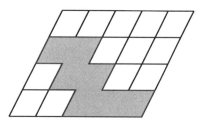

If the area of the entire figure is 80 cm², what is the area of the shaded region?

(A) 12 cm²
(B) 20 cm²
(C) 24 cm²
(D) 28 cm²

40. Sheldon is a member of the 10-student debate club. One of the ten students is randomly selected as the secretary, then one of the ten students is randomly selected as treasurer. What is the probability that Sheldon is selected as both secretary and treasurer?

(A) $\dfrac{1}{9}$

(B) $\dfrac{1}{10}$

(C) $\dfrac{1}{90}$

(D) $\dfrac{1}{100}$

41. The figure shows a square inscribed in a circle.

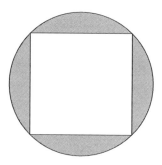

If the area of the square is 16 square units, what is the area of the shaded region?

(A) 4 square units
(B) 8 square units
(C) $8\pi - 8$ square units
(D) $8\pi - 16$ square units

42. Julia collected data for a science project and recorded it on the following stem and leaf plot.

| Stem | Leaf | | | | | |
|------|---|---|---|---|---|---|
| 4 | 0 | 3 | 5 | | | |
| 5 | 1 | 1 | 5 | 6 | | |
| 6 | 2 | 2 | 3 | 5 | 8 | 8 |
| 7 | 4 | 4 | 4 | 5 | | |
| 8 | 1 | 5 | | | | |
| 9 | 0 | 3 | 3 | 5 | | |

What is the mode of Julia's data?

(A) 55
(B) 62
(C) 68
(D) 74

**STOP. If there is time, you may check your work in this section only.** STOP

# Essay Directions

There is an essay topic printed on the next page of this test. Do not turn the page until you are told to begin. Once you are told to begin, you will have 30 minutes to write an essay on the topic provided. You may not write on another topic.

Your writing should be as clear as possible. The quality of your writing is more important than the length of your essay, but your essay should be long enough to develop your ideas and to demonstrate your writing ability.

You may plan your response in the notes section provided on the next page. Any writing you do in the notes section will NOT be counted as part of your essay. Your final draft must be written on the lined portion of your answer sheet. Only what is written on your answer sheet will be considered part of your essay. Remember that you will have only 30 minutes to plan and write your essay, so you should leave enough time to copy your final draft to the answer sheet.

Please use a blue or black pen to write your essay. Do not write outside of the box provided on the answer sheet. You may write in cursive or in print.

Please copy the following topic onto the first few lines of your answer sheet.

# Essay Topic

**Identify an object that is important to you and explain its significance.**

- Do not write on any other topic.
- Write your final draft on the answer sheet, NOT in the space below.
- Write in blue or black pen.

## Notes

_____

_____

_____

_____

_____

_____

_____

_____

_____

_____

_____

_____

_____

_____

_____

_____

# ISEE
Independent School Entrance Exam

# Practice Test 3

# Answer Sheet

## Verbal Reasoning

| | | | |
|---|---|---|---|
| 1 Ⓐ Ⓑ Ⓒ Ⓓ | 13 Ⓐ Ⓑ Ⓒ Ⓓ | 25 Ⓐ Ⓑ Ⓒ Ⓓ |
| 2 Ⓐ Ⓑ Ⓒ Ⓓ | 14 Ⓐ Ⓑ Ⓒ Ⓓ | 26 Ⓐ Ⓑ Ⓒ Ⓓ |
| 3 Ⓐ Ⓑ Ⓒ Ⓓ | 15 Ⓐ Ⓑ Ⓒ Ⓓ | 27 Ⓐ Ⓑ Ⓒ Ⓓ |
| 4 Ⓐ Ⓑ Ⓒ Ⓓ | 16 Ⓐ Ⓑ Ⓒ Ⓓ | 28 Ⓐ Ⓑ Ⓒ Ⓓ |
| 5 Ⓐ Ⓑ Ⓒ Ⓓ | 17 Ⓐ Ⓑ Ⓒ Ⓓ | 29 Ⓐ Ⓑ Ⓒ Ⓓ |
| 6 Ⓐ Ⓑ Ⓒ Ⓓ | 18 Ⓐ Ⓑ Ⓒ Ⓓ | 30 Ⓐ Ⓑ Ⓒ Ⓓ |
| 7 Ⓐ Ⓑ Ⓒ Ⓓ | 19 Ⓐ Ⓑ Ⓒ Ⓓ | 31 Ⓐ Ⓑ Ⓒ Ⓓ |
| 8 Ⓐ Ⓑ Ⓒ Ⓓ | 20 Ⓐ Ⓑ Ⓒ Ⓓ | 32 Ⓐ Ⓑ Ⓒ Ⓓ |
| 9 Ⓐ Ⓑ Ⓒ Ⓓ | 21 Ⓐ Ⓑ Ⓒ Ⓓ | 33 Ⓐ Ⓑ Ⓒ Ⓓ |
| 10 Ⓐ Ⓑ Ⓒ Ⓓ | 22 Ⓐ Ⓑ Ⓒ Ⓓ | 34 Ⓐ Ⓑ Ⓒ Ⓓ |
| 11 Ⓐ Ⓑ Ⓒ Ⓓ | 23 Ⓐ Ⓑ Ⓒ Ⓓ | 35 Ⓐ Ⓑ Ⓒ Ⓓ |
| 12 Ⓐ Ⓑ Ⓒ Ⓓ | 24 Ⓐ Ⓑ Ⓒ Ⓓ | |

## Quantitative Reasoning

| | | | |
|---|---|---|---|
| 1 Ⓐ Ⓑ Ⓒ Ⓓ | 12 Ⓐ Ⓑ Ⓒ Ⓓ | 23 Ⓐ Ⓑ Ⓒ Ⓓ |
| 2 Ⓐ Ⓑ Ⓒ Ⓓ | 13 Ⓐ Ⓑ Ⓒ Ⓓ | 24 Ⓐ Ⓑ Ⓒ Ⓓ |
| 3 Ⓐ Ⓑ Ⓒ Ⓓ | 14 Ⓐ Ⓑ Ⓒ Ⓓ | 25 Ⓐ Ⓑ Ⓒ Ⓓ |
| 4 Ⓐ Ⓑ Ⓒ Ⓓ | 15 Ⓐ Ⓑ Ⓒ Ⓓ | 26 Ⓐ Ⓑ Ⓒ Ⓓ |
| 5 Ⓐ Ⓑ Ⓒ Ⓓ | 16 Ⓐ Ⓑ Ⓒ Ⓓ | 27 Ⓐ Ⓑ Ⓒ Ⓓ |
| 6 Ⓐ Ⓑ Ⓒ Ⓓ | 17 Ⓐ Ⓑ Ⓒ Ⓓ | 28 Ⓐ Ⓑ Ⓒ Ⓓ |
| 7 Ⓐ Ⓑ Ⓒ Ⓓ | 18 Ⓐ Ⓑ Ⓒ Ⓓ | 29 Ⓐ Ⓑ Ⓒ Ⓓ |
| 8 Ⓐ Ⓑ Ⓒ Ⓓ | 19 Ⓐ Ⓑ Ⓒ Ⓓ | 30 Ⓐ Ⓑ Ⓒ Ⓓ |
| 9 Ⓐ Ⓑ Ⓒ Ⓓ | 20 Ⓐ Ⓑ Ⓒ Ⓓ | 31 Ⓐ Ⓑ Ⓒ Ⓓ |
| 10 Ⓐ Ⓑ Ⓒ Ⓓ | 21 Ⓐ Ⓑ Ⓒ Ⓓ | 32 Ⓐ Ⓑ Ⓒ Ⓓ |
| 11 Ⓐ Ⓑ Ⓒ Ⓓ | 22 Ⓐ Ⓑ Ⓒ Ⓓ | |

## Reading Comprehension

| | | | |
|---|---|---|---|
| 1 Ⓐ Ⓑ Ⓒ Ⓓ | 11 Ⓐ Ⓑ Ⓒ Ⓓ | 21 Ⓐ Ⓑ Ⓒ Ⓓ |
| 2 Ⓐ Ⓑ Ⓒ Ⓓ | 12 Ⓐ Ⓑ Ⓒ Ⓓ | 22 Ⓐ Ⓑ Ⓒ Ⓓ |
| 3 Ⓐ Ⓑ Ⓒ Ⓓ | 13 Ⓐ Ⓑ Ⓒ Ⓓ | 23 Ⓐ Ⓑ Ⓒ Ⓓ |
| 4 Ⓐ Ⓑ Ⓒ Ⓓ | 14 Ⓐ Ⓑ Ⓒ Ⓓ | 24 Ⓐ Ⓑ Ⓒ Ⓓ |
| 5 Ⓐ Ⓑ Ⓒ Ⓓ | 15 Ⓐ Ⓑ Ⓒ Ⓓ | 25 Ⓐ Ⓑ Ⓒ Ⓓ |
| 6 Ⓐ Ⓑ Ⓒ Ⓓ | 16 Ⓐ Ⓑ Ⓒ Ⓓ | 26 Ⓐ Ⓑ Ⓒ Ⓓ |
| 7 Ⓐ Ⓑ Ⓒ Ⓓ | 17 Ⓐ Ⓑ Ⓒ Ⓓ | 27 Ⓐ Ⓑ Ⓒ Ⓓ |
| 8 Ⓐ Ⓑ Ⓒ Ⓓ | 18 Ⓐ Ⓑ Ⓒ Ⓓ | 28 Ⓐ Ⓑ Ⓒ Ⓓ |
| 9 Ⓐ Ⓑ Ⓒ Ⓓ | 19 Ⓐ Ⓑ Ⓒ Ⓓ | 29 Ⓐ Ⓑ Ⓒ Ⓓ |
| 10 Ⓐ Ⓑ Ⓒ Ⓓ | 20 Ⓐ Ⓑ Ⓒ Ⓓ | 30 Ⓐ Ⓑ Ⓒ Ⓓ |

## Mathematics Achievement

| | | | |
|---|---|---|---|
| 1 Ⓐ Ⓑ Ⓒ Ⓓ | 15 Ⓐ Ⓑ Ⓒ Ⓓ | 29 Ⓐ Ⓑ Ⓒ Ⓓ |
| 2 Ⓐ Ⓑ Ⓒ Ⓓ | 16 Ⓐ Ⓑ Ⓒ Ⓓ | 30 Ⓐ Ⓑ Ⓒ Ⓓ |
| 3 Ⓐ Ⓑ Ⓒ Ⓓ | 17 Ⓐ Ⓑ Ⓒ Ⓓ | 31 Ⓐ Ⓑ Ⓒ Ⓓ |
| 4 Ⓐ Ⓑ Ⓒ Ⓓ | 18 Ⓐ Ⓑ Ⓒ Ⓓ | 32 Ⓐ Ⓑ Ⓒ Ⓓ |
| 5 Ⓐ Ⓑ Ⓒ Ⓓ | 19 Ⓐ Ⓑ Ⓒ Ⓓ | 33 Ⓐ Ⓑ Ⓒ Ⓓ |
| 6 Ⓐ Ⓑ Ⓒ Ⓓ | 20 Ⓐ Ⓑ Ⓒ Ⓓ | 34 Ⓐ Ⓑ Ⓒ Ⓓ |
| 7 Ⓐ Ⓑ Ⓒ Ⓓ | 21 Ⓐ Ⓑ Ⓒ Ⓓ | 35 Ⓐ Ⓑ Ⓒ Ⓓ |
| 8 Ⓐ Ⓑ Ⓒ Ⓓ | 22 Ⓐ Ⓑ Ⓒ Ⓓ | 36 Ⓐ Ⓑ Ⓒ Ⓓ |
| 9 Ⓐ Ⓑ Ⓒ Ⓓ | 23 Ⓐ Ⓑ Ⓒ Ⓓ | 37 Ⓐ Ⓑ Ⓒ Ⓓ |
| 10 Ⓐ Ⓑ Ⓒ Ⓓ | 24 Ⓐ Ⓑ Ⓒ Ⓓ | 38 Ⓐ Ⓑ Ⓒ Ⓓ |
| 11 Ⓐ Ⓑ Ⓒ Ⓓ | 25 Ⓐ Ⓑ Ⓒ Ⓓ | 39 Ⓐ Ⓑ Ⓒ Ⓓ |
| 12 Ⓐ Ⓑ Ⓒ Ⓓ | 26 Ⓐ Ⓑ Ⓒ Ⓓ | 40 Ⓐ Ⓑ Ⓒ Ⓓ |
| 13 Ⓐ Ⓑ Ⓒ Ⓓ | 27 Ⓐ Ⓑ Ⓒ Ⓓ | 41 Ⓐ Ⓑ Ⓒ Ⓓ |
| 14 Ⓐ Ⓑ Ⓒ Ⓓ | 28 Ⓐ Ⓑ Ⓒ Ⓓ | 42 Ⓐ Ⓑ Ⓒ Ⓓ |

# Answer Sheet - Essay

Write your response in blue or black pen.

STUDENT NAME _____

| Write your essay topic here. |
| --- |
| _____ |
| _____ |
| _____ |

Write your response here.

_____

_____

_____

_____

_____

_____

_____

_____

_____

_____

_____

_____

_____

_____

_____

_____

_____

_____

_____

_____

_____

_____

_____

_____

_____

_____

_____

(Answer Sheet - Essay continued)

# ISEE
Independent School Entrance Exam

# Upper Level
# Verbal Reasoning

# Practice Test 3

*This page intentionally left blank.*

# Section 1
# Verbal Reasoning

| **35 Questions** | **Time: 17.5 minutes** |
|---|---|

This section is divided into two parts that contain two different types of questions. As soon as you have completed Part One, answer the questions in Part Two. You may write in your test booklet. For each answer you select, fill in the corresponding circle on your answer document.

## Part One — Synonyms

Each question in Part One consists of a word in capital letters followed by four answer choices. Select the one word that is most nearly the same in meaning as the word in capital letters.

---

SAMPLE QUESTION:                                    SAMPLE ANSWER:

   EXTEND:                                          Ⓐ ● Ⓒ Ⓓ

   (A) avoid
   (B) lengthen
   (C) criticize
   (D) discover

---

## Part Two — Sentence Completion

Each question in Part Two is made up of a sentence with one or two blanks. One blank indicates that one word is missing. Two blanks indicate that two words are missing. Each sentence is followed by four answer choices. Select the one word or pair of words that best completes the meaning of the sentence as a whole.

---

SAMPLE QUESTIONS:                                   SAMPLE ANSWERS:

   Unlike her older brother, who always acted --------,      ● Ⓑ Ⓒ Ⓓ
   Cheryl preferred to take her time.

   (A) quickly
   (B) carefully
   (C) stupidly
   (D) wisely


   Whitewater rafting is both ------- and dangerous: rapids     Ⓐ Ⓑ Ⓒ ●
   may provide thrills, but they also threaten a rafter's ------.

   (A) ancient...pride
   (B) understandable...judgment
   (C) informative...freedom
   (D) exciting...safety

---

STOP. Do not go on until told to do so. **STOP**

# Part One — Synonyms

**Directions:** Select the word that is most nearly the same in meaning as the word in capital letters.

1. CONCLUDE:

   (A)  remember
   (B)  develop
   (C)  format
   (D)  finish

2. WEARY:

   (A)  tired
   (B)  concerned
   (C)  healthy
   (D)  hardened

3. COAX:

   (A)  pretend
   (B)  suspend
   (C)  deceive
   (D)  persuade

4. EXHIBIT:

   (A)  study
   (B)  locate
   (C)  show
   (D)  worsen

5. PROCRASTINATE:

   (A)  ignore
   (B)  quit
   (C)  delay
   (D)  drift

6. REVOLTING:

   (A)  sickening
   (B)  aggressive
   (C)  slippery
   (D)  troubling

7. PETRIFY:

   (A)  focus
   (B)  frighten
   (C)  thaw
   (D)  enlarge

8. CRITERION:

   (A)  standard
   (B)  performance
   (C)  analysis
   (D)  disapproval

9. ILLICIT:

   (A)  prohibited
   (B)  invisible
   (C)  quiet
   (D)  uncommon

10. TRAIT:

   (A)  passion
   (B)  instinct
   (C)  feature
   (D)  flaw

11. DISTRAUGHT:

(A) educated
(B) tight
(C) doubtful
(D) worried

12. PLIABLE:

(A) applicable
(B) elastic
(C) layered
(D) relaxed

13. ACCLAIM:

(A) request
(B) praise
(C) insist
(D) command

14. DESPONDENT:

(A) connected
(B) poor
(C) depressed
(D) hesitant

15. FRUGAL:

(A) cheap
(B) dependent
(C) hungry
(D) royal

16. TORRENT:

(A) oven
(B) flood
(C) separator
(D) content

17. VERBATIM:

(A) actively
(B) normally
(C) confidently
(D) precisely

## Part Two — Sentence Completion

**Directions:** Select the word or word pair that best completes the sentence.

18. Because Mr. Goldstein had never been fond of lengthy essays, he gave his writing students high marks for -------.

    (A) wordiness
    (B) cleverness
    (C) brevity
    (D) awkwardness

19. Even when not on stage, operatic baritone Thomas Hampson speaks in ------- tones that resonate throughout the room.

    (A) gentle
    (B) sonorous
    (C) hushed
    (D) eloquent

20. When protestors took to the streets, blocked cars from passing, and blasted their message through loud megaphones, the police were sent to quiet the -------.

    (A) disturbance
    (B) enigma
    (C) dominance
    (D) simulation

21. Prior to the Civil War, the network of hideouts and helpers known as the Underground Railroad helped shuttle African American slaves from ------- to freedom.

    (A) privilege
    (B) luxury
    (C) anarchy
    (D) bondage

22. Though she was initially reluctant to beg, Erin eventually broke down and ------- her father to send her to summer camp.

    (A) forced
    (B) compelled
    (C) instructed
    (D) implored

23. The new comedy was praised for its dynamic, captivating dialogue, which contrasted sharply with the ------- exchanges that are the hallmark of its genre.

    (A) enthralling
    (B) covert
    (C) amusing
    (D) bland

24. A great ------- caught the ship's crew by surprise, and they hurried to secure items on deck against the crashing waves and howling wind.

    (A) transformation
    (B) tempest
    (C) conquest
    (D) forecast

25. North and South America are named for Amerigo Vespucci, a 15ᵗʰ century ------- whose maps of Brazil and the West Indies helped establish that these land masses were not in fact part of Asia.

    (A) cartographer
    (B) economist
    (C) architect
    (D) philosopher

26. Laura preferred to let her children resolve disputes among themselves, but from time to time she had to -------.

    (A) ponder
    (B) detach
    (C) intervene
    (D) socialize

27. The loud complaints that accompany the enforcement of new regulations generally ------- as time passes and people get used to the rules.

    (A) intensify
    (B) contract
    (C) subside
    (D) realign

28. Volcanic eruptions are often ------- by minor earthquakes that ------- the coming explosion.

    (A) heralded...conceal
    (B) preceded...foreshadow
    (C) indicated...irradiate
    (D) prevented...enable

29. The soldiers had almost no bread, meat, or other -------, so the situation at Valley Forge in the winter of 1778 was very -------.

    (A) provisions...grim
    (B) supplies...flexible
    (C) essentials...secure
    (D) shelter...perilous

30. To ------- the popular misconception that girls are less talented in math than boys, the National Council of Teachers of Mathematics ------- a program to celebrate women's achievements in the field.

    (A) dispel...retracted
    (B) counter...sponsored
    (C) encourage...established
    (D) corroborate...backed

31. Although food sources are ------- on the plains in the winter, warm summer weather brings ------- game to the region.

    (A) garbled...fierce
    (B) scattered...verdant
    (C) vigilant...harmless
    (D) scarce...abundant

32. Elderly people who discover a ------- talent in their waning years don't achieve the fame of those ------- who develop exceptional abilities as young children.

    (A) hidden…imbeciles
    (B) meaningless… misfits
    (C) latent…prodigies
    (D) precocious…innovators

33. Learning calculus is a ------- task even with excellent instruction; studying it independently is even more -------.

    (A) formidable…enticing
    (B) proficient…taxing
    (C) problematic…straightforward
    (D) challenging…daunting

34. Each April, residents of Greenfield ------- the picket fences that line their properties; these ------- repairs are necessary because of ice damage sustained during the winter.

    (A) mend…annual
    (B) erect…oppressive
    (C) examine…redundant
    (D) relay…tedious

35. South Africans ------- Nelson Mandela as a ------- national hero who insisted on change despite repeated threats to his personal safety.

    (A) regard…ravenous
    (B) revere…courageous
    (C) deride…precious
    (D) interpret…wary

STOP. Do not go on until told to do so. STOP

# ISEE
Independent School Entrance Exam

# Upper Level
# Quantitative Reasoning

# Practice Test 3

# Section 2
# Quantitative Reasoning

---

| 32 Questions | Time: 30 minutes |
| --- | --- |

This section has two parts that contain two different kinds of questions. Do not pause after Part One. Continue working through Part Two. You may write in your test booklet.

Letters such as $x$ and $y$ stand for real numbers. All figures are drawn to scale unless otherwise stated.

**Part One — Word Problems**

Each question in Part One consists of a word problem followed by four answer choices. Select the best answer from the four choices given and fill in the corresponding circle on your answer document.

---

EXAMPLE 1:                                              SAMPLE ANSWER

Ⓐ Ⓑ Ⓒ ●

Which of the following fractions is greater than $\frac{3}{4}$?

(A) $\frac{1}{5}$

(B) $\frac{1}{4}$

(C) $\frac{2}{5}$

(D) $\frac{4}{5}$

The correct answer is $\frac{4}{5}$, so circle D is darkened.

---

     *Go on to the next page.* ➡

# QR

**Part Two — Quantitative Comparisons**

In Part Two, use the given information to compare the quantities given in Column A and Column B.
Choose one of these four answer choices:

        (A)  The quantity in Column A is greater.
        (B)  The quantity in Column B is greater.
        (C)  The two quantities are equal.
        (D)  The relationship cannot be determined from the information given.

---

**EXAMPLE 2:**

SAMPLE ANSWER

Ⓐ Ⓑ ● Ⓓ

| Column A | Column B |
|---|---|
| The greatest integer that is less than 4.1 | The smallest integer that is greater than 3.9 |

The quantity in Column A (4) is the same as the quantity in Column B (4), so circle C is darkened.

---

**EXAMPLE 3:**

SAMPLE ANSWER

Ⓐ Ⓑ Ⓒ ●

$$x^2 > 4$$

| Column A | Column B |
|---|---|
| $x$ | 2 |

One possible value for $x$ is 3 because $3^2 = 9$ and $9 > 4$. Another possible value for $x$ is $-3$ because $(-3)^2 = 9$ also. Because the quantity in Column A (3 or $-3$, for instance) may be greater than or less than the quantity in Column B (2), the relationship cannot be determined and circle D is darkened.

STOP. Do not go on until told to do so. **STOP**

## Part One — Word Problems

**Directions:** Choose the best answer from the four choices given.

1. Triangle ABC is similar to triangle DEF.

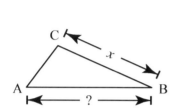
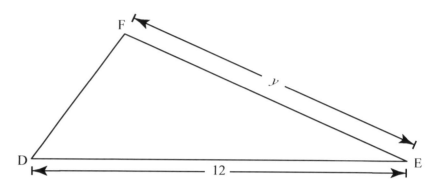

   If $\frac{y}{x} = 3$, what is the length of side $\overline{AB}$?

   (A) 3
   (B) 4
   (C) 5
   (D) 6

---

2. If $y = \sqrt{8 - x}$ and $x \geq 4$, what is the minimum possible value for y?

   (A) $2\sqrt{2}$
   (B) 2
   (C) 0
   (D) There is no minimum value for y

3. If $\triangle x = x^2 + 1$, what is the value of $\triangle 7 - \triangle 5$?

   (A) 5
   (B) 9
   (C) 24
   (D) 28

4. If $(a - b)^2 - 9 = 0$ and $a > b > 0$, which of the following expressions is equal to $a$?

   (A) $\sqrt{9 + b^2}$
   (B) $\sqrt{9 - b^2}$
   (C) $b + 3$
   (D) $b - 3$

5. What is the value of the expression below?

$$\frac{(2^2 \times 3 + 12) \times 2}{32 \times 9}$$

(A) $\frac{1}{6}$

(B) $\frac{1}{3}$

(C) $\frac{3}{8}$

(D) $\frac{5}{12}$

6. The radius of a circle is decreased by 10%. What is the percent decrease in the area of the circle?

(A) 10%

(B) 19%

(C) 20%

(D) 21%

7. Eliot throws a number cube labeled with the numbers 1 through 6 six hundred times. He makes a red tally mark on a piece of paper for each roll that results in a number less than 4 and a blue tally mark for roll that results in a 6. Otherwise he makes no tally mark. Of the following possible counts of the tally marks, which is most likely?

(A) 308 red; 98 blue

(B) 402 red; 104 blue

(C) 150 red; 100 blue

(D) 320 red; 280 blue

8. The circle graph below represents the nationalities of the 24,000 spectators at a soccer tournament.

Spectators at a Soccer Tournament
(24,000 total)

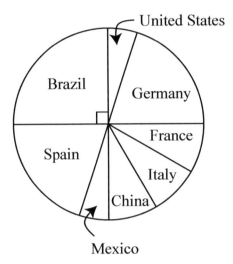

There are equal numbers of spectators from China, France, and Italy. How many nations have more than 3000 spectators at the tournament?

(A) 1

(B) 2

(C) 3

(D) 6

9. If $a$ is an odd integer, which of the following MUST be an integer?

(A) $\frac{a}{2} + \frac{1}{2}$

(B) $\frac{a}{3} + \frac{1}{3}$

(C) $\frac{a}{3} + \frac{2}{3}$

(D) $\frac{a}{4} + \frac{3}{4}$

10. If $m$ and $n$ are positive integers and $2x(5x + 3y) = mx^2 + nxy$, what is the value of $m - n$?

(A) $-4$
(B) $-1$
(C) $1$
(D) $4$

11. Let $z$ be defined as follows:

$$z = \frac{1}{2} \times \frac{1}{4} \times \frac{1}{8}$$

What is the value of $2^9 \times z$ ?

(A) $\dfrac{1}{2^6}$
(B) $\dfrac{1}{2^5}$
(C) $2$
(D) $2^3$

12. Celine was given a list of values and asked to make a bar graph of the frequency of the values. She began the bar graph below but forgot to include the column for the value 11.

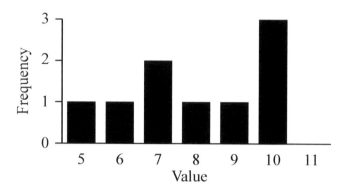

If the correct median of the list is 9, how many times does the value 11 appear in the list?

(A) once
(B) twice
(C) three times
(D) four times

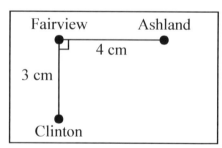

13. Ashland is east of Fairview, and Clinton is south of Fairview. If one centimeter on the scale map above represents four kilometers, what is the distance from Ashland to Clinton?

(A) 16 kilometers
(B) 20 kilometers
(C) 28 kilometers
(D) 48 kilometers

14. The figure shows a pyramid with a square base. Its four sides are equilateral triangles.

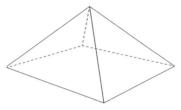

Which of the following could NOT be a net of the pyramid?

(A)

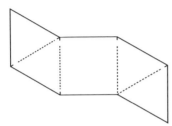

(B)

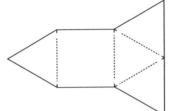

(C)

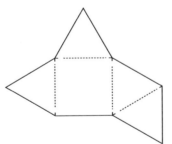

(D)

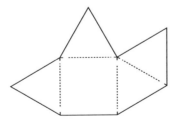

15. The population of Springfield changed over the past year as new residents moved in and other residents left. The solid line represents the rate at which residents left Springfield and the dashed line represents the rate at which new residents moved in.

Springfield's Changing Population

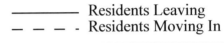

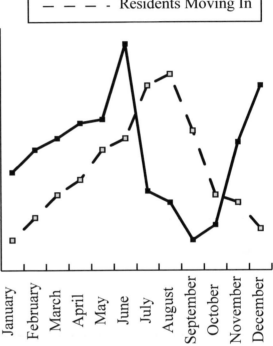

During which months was the population of Springfield growing?

(A) January through June
(B) January through August
(C) July through October
(D) September through December

16. Shanice has a list of 11 consecutive integers. The median of the list is 14. Shanice then makes a new list by subtracting two from each number in her original list. Which of the following is a number in the new list?

   (A) 6
   (B) 7
   (C) 18
   (D) 29

17. If $a$ and $b$ are prime numbers, which of the following must be a factor of $\dfrac{100a^2b}{20a}$ ?

   (A) $5a^2$
   (B) $35b$
   (C) $10a$
   (D) $5b$

18. Ally and Meg are both assigned to read a short story, but they don't know exactly how long it is. Meg claims that she can read the story in half the time that Ally can. Which one piece of additional information would be needed to determine whether Meg is correct?

   (A) The sum of the rates at which Meg and Ally read
   (B) The difference between the rates at which Meg and Ally read
   (C) The ratio of the rates at which Meg and Ally read
   (D) The product of the rates at which Meg and Ally read

## Part Two—Quantitative Comparisons

**Directions:** Using the information given in each question, compare the quantity in Column A to the quantity in Column B. All questions in Part Two have these answer choices:

(A)　The quantity in Column A is greater.
(B)　The quantity in Column B is greater.
(C)　The two quantities are equal.
(D)　The relationship cannot be determined from the information given.

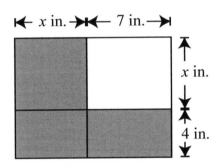

|  | Column A | Column B |
|---|---|---|
| 19. | The shaded area | $x^2 + 7x + 28$ inches$^2$ |

A coin is flipped 5 times in row.

|  | Column A | Column B |
|---|---|---|
| 20. | If the first four flips come up heads, the probability that the last flip is tails. | If the first four flips come up tails, the probability that the last flip is tails. |

|  | Column A | Column B |
|---|---|---|
| 21. | $(3-2) \times 5 + 4 \times (2+1)$ | 27 |

Riverside and Jamestown had the same population in 2009. The population of Jamestown decreased by 8% from 2009 to 2010 and decreased by 8% again from 2010 to 2011. Riverside's population did not change from 2009 to 2010, but it decreased by 16% from 2010 to 2011.

|  | Column A | Column B |
|---|---|---|
| 22. | The population of Jamestown in 2011 | The population of Riverside in 2011 |

$$y = x + 2$$

|  | Column A | Column B |
|---|---|---|
| 23. | $4(x+2)$ | $2(x+y)$ |

|  | Column A | Column B |
|---|---|---|
| 24. | $(x+y)^2 - 16$ | $(x+y-2)(x+y+2)$ |

|  | Column A | Column B |
|---|---|---|
| 25. | $(-2)^6$ | $(-2)^9$ |

**Answer choices for all questions on this page:**

(A) The quantity in Column A is greater.
(B) The quantity in Column B is greater.
(C) The two quantities are equal.
(D) The relationship cannot be determined from the information given.

The area of a rectangle is 36 square inches.

| | Column A | Column B |
|---|---|---|
| 26. | The perimeter of the rectangle | 72 inches |

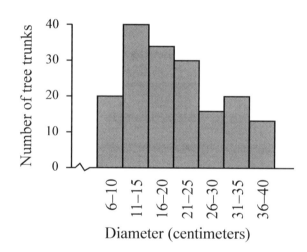

The histogram above shows the diameters of tree trunks in a section of forest.

| | Column A | Column B |
|---|---|---|
| 27. | The range of the diameters | 30 centimeters |

Square S

Triangle T

Note: Figures not drawn to scale

Triangle T is isosceles. The area of Triangle T is 5.5 and the area of Square S is 11.

| | Column A | Column B |
|---|---|---|
| 28. | The perimeter of Square S | The perimeter of Triangle T |

A jar contains 5 marbles: 1 red marble and 4 blue marbles. One marble is drawn at random, then a second marble is drawn without replacing the first.

| | Column A | Column B |
|---|---|---|
| 29. | The probability that at least one marble drawn is blue | $\frac{4}{5}$ |

---

**Answer choices for all questions on this page:**

    (A) The quantity in Column A is greater.
    (B) The quantity in Column B is greater.
    (C) The two quantities are equal.
    (D) The relationship cannot be determined from the information given.

---

A movie ticket costs $15.00 and a ticket to a baseball game costs $45.00. George attends three times as many movies this year as he does baseball games.

| Column A | Column B |
|---|---|
| 30. The amount George spends on movie tickets this year | The amount George spends on tickets to baseball games this year |

---

A rectangular enclosure is formed by using 24 feet of fencing.

| Column A | Column B |
|---|---|
| 31. The distance between diagonally opposite corners of the enclosure | 10 feet |

Line $k$ contains points in the second and fourth quadrants. Line $j$ contains points in the first and third quadrants.

| Column A | Column B |
|---|---|
| 32. The slope of line $k$ | The slope of line $j$ |

STOP. If there is time, you may check your work in this section only.

**STOP**

*This page intentionally left blank.*

# ISEE
Independent School Entrance Exam

# Upper Level
# Reading Comprehension

# Practice Test 3

*This page intentionally left blank.*

# Section 3
## Reading Comprehension

This section contains five short reading passages. Each passage is followed by six questions based on its content. Answer the questions following each passage on the basis of what is stated or implied in that passage. You may write in your test booklet.

STOP. Do not go on
until told to do so.

STOP

Questions 1–6

1    In 1996, the United States was perhaps
2  the worldwide leader in consumer internet
3  access. Not only did recently-founded internet
4  companies offer telephone-based connections
5  (albeit very slow ones) to more than 90% of
6  households, but other pioneers were leading the
7  push into broadband: fast internet connections
8  that would change the way we interact with the
9  world around us.
10    Somewhere between then and now we
11  lost momentum. Other developed nations
12  have leapt past the United States in broadband
13  connectivity, according to a 2012 report by the
14  Federal Communications Commission, which
15  ranked the U.S. as 24th in average broadband
16  speed among the countries surveyed. To add
17  insult to injury, broadband in the U.S. ranks as
18  some of the most expensive internet access in
19  the world.
20    We, as consumers of outdated and
21  overpriced technology, often do not know what
22  we are missing, simply because no alternatives
23  exist. It is not unusual for there to be only
24  one provider of broadband internet access in
25  a neighborhood, or even in an entire city or
26  region. This is in part due to the large capital
27  investment needed to build a network capable
28  of reaching most homes in an area. But in
29  addition, many companies have little interest
30  in a low-profit-margin business like broadband
31  internet access.
32    Whatever the cause, the effect is a lack of

33  competition that is hurting consumers. When
34  a cable internet provider is the only game
35  in town, it has no incentive to provide high
36  quality service. Customers will purchase its
37  mediocre product anyway. After all, second-
38  rate broadband is better than no broadband at
39  all.
40    Recent entries into the market offer a
41  glimmer of hope. At least two major American
42  companies have recently begun providing home
43  internet access via fiber-optic cables, which can
44  carry substantially more data than the traditional
45  copper wire deployed by most cable companies.
46  The services are not yet widely available, but
47  the sleepy cable giants who have until now
48  dominated the broadband market are sitting
49  up and taking notice. Already, some of these
50  plodding dinosaurs have slashed prices and
51  increased access speeds in areas where fiber-
52  optic competition has been introduced.
53    Adding to the pressure on entrenched
54  broadband providers is the explosion of
55  wireless broadband connections over cellular
56  smartphones. Lately, consumers have
57  discovered that their phones often provide
58  internet speeds that are as fast as, if not faster
59  than, the speeds of their wired broadband
60  connections at home. The rapid advances in
61  wireless technology have awoken the masses to
62  the possibility that they have been duped; their
63  supposedly speedy wired connections are in fact
64  fossils from a bygone age of clumsy technology.

1. The main idea of the passage is that

   (A) the United States is currently a world leader in consumer internet access
   (B) internet access in the United States has not improved since 1996
   (C) the United States has lost its leading position in consumer internet access
   (D) cable companies have misled consumers about their internet access

2. In line 61, the word "masses" refers to

   (A) people who purchase internet access
   (B) companies who sell internet access
   (C) large quantities of data
   (D) fiber optic cables

3. The passage suggests that the author views most providers of wired internet access in the United States as

   (A) stuck in the past
   (B) slow to react to increased competition
   (C) incapable of providing faster internet access
   (D) manipulative and deceitful

4. In the second paragraph (lines 10-19), the author supports his argument by

   (A) citing an authority
   (B) listing numerous statistics
   (C) insulting U.S. broadband providers
   (D) praising other nations

5. It can be inferred from lines 49-52 that the author believes competition among providers of wired internet access is

   (A) bad for consumers because they must pay more for new products
   (B) good for consumers because they receive faster service for less money
   (C) bad for providers because consumers shift toward wireless access
   (D) good for providers because providers can charge more for their services

6. The author states that consumers purchase overpriced, low-quality wired broadband for all of the following reasons EXCEPT:

   (A) there are no other options for broadband service
   (B) consumers are unaware that the service is poor
   (C) even poor service is better than nothing
   (D) wireless service is fast but too expensive

Questions 7–12

1  President Abraham Lincoln issued the
2  Emancipation Proclamation on January 1, 1863,
3  as the nation approached its third year of bloody
4  civil war. The proclamation declared "that all
5  persons held as slaves" within the rebellious
6  states "are, and henceforward shall be free."
7  Despite this expansive wording, the
8  Emancipation Proclamation was limited in many
9  ways. It applied only to states that had seceded
10  from the Union, leaving slavery untouched
11  in the loyal border states. It also expressly
12  exempted parts of the Confederacy that had
13  already come under Northern control. Most
14  important, the freedom it promised depended
15  upon Union military victory.
16  Although the Emancipation Proclamation
17  did not end slavery in the nation, it captured
18  the hearts and imaginations of millions of
19  Americans and fundamentally transformed the
20  character of the war. After January 1, 1863,
21  every advance of federal troops expanded the
22  domain of freedom. Moreover, the Proclamation
23  announced the acceptance of black men into the
24  Union Army and Navy, enabling the liberated to
25  become liberators. By the end of the war, almost
26  200,000 black soldiers and sailors had fought
27  for the Union and freedom.
28  From the first days of the Civil War, slaves
29  had acted to secure their own liberty. The
30  Emancipation Proclamation confirmed their

31  insistence that the war for the Union must
32  become a war for freedom. It added moral force
33  to the Union cause and strengthened the Union
34  both militarily and politically. As a milestone
35  along the road to slavery's final destruction, the
36  Emancipation Proclamation has assumed a place
37  among the great documents of human freedom.
38  The original Emancipation Proclamation, is
39  in the National Archives in Washington, D.C.
40  The text covers five pages, and the document
41  was originally tied with narrow red and blue
42  ribbons, which were attached to the signature
43  page by a wafered impression of the seal of the
44  United States. Most of the ribbon remains; parts
45  of the seal are still decipherable, but other parts
46  have worn off.
47  The document was bound with other
48  proclamations in a large volume preserved for
49  many years by the Department of State. When it
50  was prepared for binding, it was reinforced with
51  strips along the center folds and then mounted
52  on a still larger sheet of heavy paper. Written in
53  red ink on the upper right-hand corner of this
54  large sheet is the number of the Proclamation,
55  95, given to it by the Department of State
56  long after it was signed. With other records,
57  the volume containing the Emancipation
58  Proclamation was transferred in 1936 from the
59  Department of State to the National Archives of
60  the United States.

7. The "domain of freedom" (line 22) refers to places where

   (A) federal troops had won military victories
   (B) slaves had secured their own liberty
   (C) the Emancipation Proclamation was in effect
   (D) slaves desired freedom

8. The last two paragraphs (lines 38-60) are primarily concerned with the

   (A) decorative parts of official papers
   (B) preservation of a physical document
   (C) decay of an object over time
   (D) bureaucracy of record-keeping

9. The passage as a whole is mostly focused on

   (A) freedom as a human right
   (B) places where files are archived
   (C) a pronouncement and its significance
   (D) decisions made by a historical person

10. The "liberators" mentioned in line 25 are

    (A) Union politicians
    (B) white Union soldiers
    (C) former slaves
    (D) freeborn black men

11. The second paragraph (lines 7-15) is organized as

    (A) a list of limitations
    (B) a narrative about a war
    (C) a series of criticisms
    (D) a description of legal terms

12. As used in line 29, the word "secure" most nearly means

    (A) protect
    (B) obtain
    (C) attach
    (D) oppose

Questions 13–18

1    I can truthfully say that my entire life
2  has been spent with cattle. I was born in the
3  Shenandoah Valley, northern Virginia, in May
4  of 1840. My father was a thrifty planter and
5  stockman, and as early as I can remember he fed
6  cattle every winter for the eastern markets. My
7  paternal Grandfather Anthony, who died before I
8  was born, was a Scotchman who had emigrated
9  to Virginia at an early age and acquired several
10  large tracts of land on an affluent of the
11  Shenandoah river.  My mother's maiden name
12  was Reed; she was of a gentle family who were
13  able to trace their forbears beyond the colonial
14  days, even to the gentry of England. Generations
15  of good birth were reflected in my mother; and
16  across a rough and eventful life I can distinctly
17  remember the refinement of her manners, her
18  courtesy to guests, her kindness to children.
19    My boyhood days were happy ones. I
20  attended a school several miles from home,
21  riding back and forth on a pony. The

22  studies were elementary, and though I never
23  distinguished myself in my classes, I was
24  always ready to race my pony, and never refused
25  to play truant when the swimming was good.
26  Evidently my father never intended any of his
27  boys for a professional career, though it was an
28  earnest hope of my mother that all of us should
29  receive a college education. My elder brother
30  and I developed business instincts early, buying
31  calves and accompanying our father on his
32  trading expeditions. Once during a vacation,
33  when we were about twelve and ten years old,
34  both of us crossed the mountains with him into
35  what is now West Virginia, where he bought
36  about two hundred young steers and drove them
37  back to our home in the valley. I must have been
38  blessed with an unfailing memory; over fifty
39  years have passed since that, my first trip from
40  home, yet I remember it vividly—can recall
41  conversations between my father and the sellers
42  as they haggled over the cattle.

13. As used in line 10, "affluent" most nearly means

    (A) wealthy
    (B) tributary
    (C) mountain
    (D) chamber

14. The passage implies that the narrator's father and mother

    (A) had different aspirations for their children
    (B) were both descended from English gentry
    (C) funded their children's business plans
    (D) traveled frequently

15. The style of the passage can best be described as

    (A) persuasive
    (B) businesslike
    (C) technical
    (D) biographical

16. According to the passage, all of the following are true of the narrator EXCEPT that he

    (A) traveled with his father
    (B) raced his pony
    (C) enjoyed swimming
    (D) did very well in school

17. The passage states that the narrator's mother had

    (A) a rough and eventful life
    (B) an unfailing memory
    (C) refined manners
    (D) Scottish ancestry

18. The passage as a whole characterizes the narrator's boyhood as

    (A) mostly happy, but tarnished by hard work
    (B) unsteady because of frequent trips
    (C) stable and pleasant
    (D) exciting and risky

Questions 19–24

1     The online image collection *Emile Berliner*
2 *and the Birth of the Recording Industry*
3 showcases the work of Emile Berliner, a
4 prominent inventor at the end of the nineteenth
5 and the beginning of the twentieth centuries.
6 Overlooked by today's historians, Berliner's
7 creative genius rivaled that of his better-known
8 contemporaries Thomas Alva Edison and
9 Alexander Graham Bell, and, like the works
10 of these two inventors, Berliner's innovations
11 helped shape the modern American way of life.
12     In America the turn of the century from
13 nineteenth to twentieth was an era of booming
14 growth. Innovation and streamlined industrial
15 processes created a large population of
16 unskilled workers in America's largest cities.
17 These changes brought about the rise of the
18 entertainment industry—and with it, sound
19 recording—as workers began to have more and
20 more leisure time. Although Emile Berliner
21 did not invent recorded sound technology, his
22 innovations led to its mass distribution.
23     Included in the Berliner collection is a
24 photograph of one of the first gramophones ever
25 built.  Berliner's flat-disc recordings, intended
26 to be played on such a gramophone, eventually
27 replaced the more fragile and unwieldy Edison
28 cylinders as consumers' sound technology of
29 choice. These early analog discs were also the

30 precursors of today's digital compact discs.
31     Also included in the collection is a
32 photograph of Berliner in his later years holding
33 a prototype of the microphone he designed. The
34 model was a vast improvement on the earlier
35 microphone used by Alexander Graham Bell for
36 his telephone systems. It is still the basic design
37 used in most microphones manufactured today.
38     In addition to his work in sound recording,
39 Berliner had a part in developing other
40 important technologies. He developed an
41 acoustic tile that helped improve audio
42 projection in older auditoriums and halls. Many
43 articles in the Berliner collection proclaim
44 how successful this invention was at the time.
45 Moreover, Berliner's technical genius was so
46 great that he was able to contribute significantly
47 to the development of the helicopter, a
48 technology unrelated to most of his earlier work.
49     Apart from his business dealings and
50 technical research, Berliner was involved in
51 philanthropic work. In 1924 he established the
52 Bureau of Health Education in Washington,
53 D.C. to disseminate health and hygiene
54 information to prevent disease. A unique item in
55 the collection is a book of rhymes, Muddy Jim,
56 published by Berliner, which advised children
57 on cleanliness and good hygiene. Berliner in
58 fact wrote the rhymes himself.

19. The passage is primarily concerned with

    (A) growth in America at the turn of the twentieth century
    (B) a collection of documents from the life of an important person
    (C) the development of sound recording technology
    (D) the rivalry among three American inventors

20. The last two paragraphs emphasize Emile Berliner's

    (A) creativity
    (B) generosity
    (C) uniqueness
    (D) versatility

21. As used in line 53, the word "disseminate" most nearly means

    (A) study
    (B) improve
    (C) validate
    (D) publicize

22. According to the passage, innovation and streamlined industrial processes

    (A) created the conditions for a new industry
    (B) caused skilled workers to lose their jobs
    (C) allowed Emile Berliner to mass-produce his products
    (D) took place exclusively in urban environments

23. The third and fourth paragraphs (lines 23-37) are similar in that they both

    (A) trace Berliner's influence on modern technology
    (B) describe photographs of Berliner
    (C) outline improvements Berliner made to Edison's designs
    (D) praise Berliner's later accomplishments

24. The author of the passage characterizes Berliner as

    (A) unappreciated in his time
    (B) more creative than many people realize
    (C) less famous today than some of his contemporaries
    (D) unable to focus his energies

Questions 25–30

1     "Downward-facing dog. Five breaths,"
2 Sudhir intoned in his soft, authoritative voice.
3     In response, 15 sets of arms pressed into the
4 ground, shifting 15 sets of hips back into the air,
5 supported by 15 pairs of feet rooted firmly to
6 the floor. I felt a release of tension in the backs
7 of my legs and a satisfying stretch through my
8 shoulders. It was good to be back.
9     Six months earlier, I had injured my right
10 quadriceps while cycling, and I hadn't been
11 to my regular yoga class since. I had missed
12 not only the physical conditioning—strength,
13 flexibility, and balance—that yoga brings to
14 my life, but also the sense of community and
15 fellowship that attends group practice. With my
16 torso upside-down and my nose in front of my
17 feet, I couldn't see any of my comrades, but I
18 could hear the telltale whisper of slow inhalation
19 and exhalation around me.
20     "Return to plank pose, keeping the fingertips
21 long and the head in line with the spine."
22 We obeyed silently, straightening our bodies
23 into single lines from head to toe, supporting
24 ourselves with straight arms and palms on
25 the floor. I felt a gentle pressure on my back:
26 Sudhir's sure hands were guiding me to a better

27 alignment. I adjusted my rib cage and allowed
28 my vertebrae to recalibrate. Another satisfying
29 release.
30     "Slowly bend your elbows no more than 90
31 degrees. Chaturanga."
32     This pose is often difficult for older women
33 like me. It requires simultaneous strength in the
34 triceps, chest and abdomen as well as active use
35 of the legs. I lowered myself carefully toward
36 my mat, slowly exhaling to counteract the
37 growing tension in my arms. Then I was there:
38 balanced, relaxed and ready to continue.
39 "Continue to upward-facing dog, rolling over
40 the toes to support yourself on the tops of the
41 feet."
42     As I lifted my chest and head, the room
43 came into focus in front of me. There was
44 Eleanor, struggling a bit with her form as
45 always; Margaret, her mid-section expanding
46 in the fourth month of pregnancy; Chazz,
47 earnest but overly conscious of his body's
48 shortcomings; Mac, hairy and muscled and
49 seemingly out of place in jeans and a baseball
50 cap. We were a mixed company, but a company
51 nonetheless, and I smiled at our incongruities.

25. The passage is mainly concerned with which of the following?

    (A) Sudhir's firm but gentle style of yoga instruction
    (B) how to correctly perform various movements in yoga
    (C) the feelings of personal satisfaction and group belonging that yoga gives the narrator
    (D) the variety of people who attend yoga class with the narrator

26. Which of the following best describes the overall organization of the passage?

    (A) Personal narrative is periodically interrupted by quotations.
    (B) Instructions for movement are presented, then ignored.
    (C) A story is told in chronological order.
    (D) The author's movement is contrasted with the movement of other participants.

27. The narrator's attitude toward the other participants in the class is best described as

    (A) uncertain
    (B) disdainful
    (C) impressed
    (D) appreciative

28. The author mentions the "slow inhalation and exhalation" around her (lines 18-19) in order to emphasize the

    (A) difficulty of executing the movements requested by Sudhir
    (B) spirit of companionship among the class participants
    (C) calm concentration associated with yoga
    (D) simultaneous nature of an activity

29. The narrator reacts to Sudhir's guiding hands by

    (A) resisting the pressure of his hands
    (B) adjusting her body in a satisfying way
    (C) exhaling slowly to counteract tension
    (D) lifting her head and chest to see those around her

30. The number 15 is repeated in lines 3-5 in order to

    (A) confirm that the narrator is not alone
    (B) show that the narrator has counted the people in the class
    (C) express concern that the class may be too crowded
    (D) emphasize that a motion is performed in unison

STOP. If there is time, you may check your work on this section only.

**STOP**

*This page intentionally left blank.*

# ISEE
## Independent School Entrance Exam

# Upper Level
# Mathematics Achievement

# Practice Test 3

*This page intentionally left blank.*

# MA

## Section 4
## Mathematics Achievement

42 Questions

Time: 36 minutes

Choose the best answer from the four choices given.  Fill in the corresponding circle on your answer document.  You may write in the test booklet.

SAMPLE QUESTION:

SAMPLE ANSWER

What number is 40% of 50?

Ⓐ ● Ⓒ Ⓓ

(A)  10
(B)  20
(C)  30
(D)  40

The correct answer is 20, so circle B is darkened.

STOP.  Do not go on
until told to do so.

STOP

1.  What is the value of the numerical expression $(3+4+5)^2$?

    (A) 24
    (B) 32
    (C) 50
    (D) 144

2.  The bar graph below shows the number of points scored in a game by the ten players on a basketball team.

    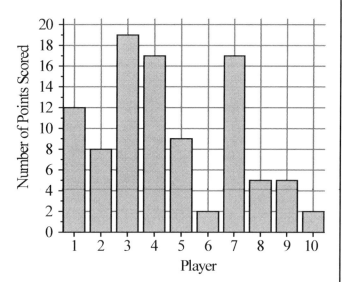

    The team scored 96 points altogether. What is the difference between the mean of the data and the median of the data?

    (A) 0.0
    (B) 0.6
    (C) 1.1
    (D) 1.6

3.  A bin contains 7 red golf balls and 9 blue golf balls. Marta, Joel and Tyrone each select a different ball from the bin without replacement. What is the probability that all 3 balls are red?

    (A) $\frac{7}{16} \times \frac{7}{15} \times \frac{7}{14}$

    (B) $\frac{7}{16} \times \frac{6}{15} \times \frac{5}{14}$

    (C) $\frac{7}{16} \times \frac{6}{16} \times \frac{5}{16}$

    (D) $\frac{7}{16} \times \frac{8}{15} \times \frac{9}{16}$

4.  Which expression is equivalent to the expression $(4p^2q^4)(6p^6q^2)$?

    (A) $(2pq^2)(12p^{12}q^4)$
    (B) $(pq)(24p^7q^5)$
    (C) $(3pq^3)(7p^7q^3)$
    (D) $(8p^4q^8)(3p^3q)$

5.  How many common factors do 30 and 36 have?

    (A) 2
    (B) 3
    (C) 4
    (D) 5

6.  Which gives all values of $x$ for which $|x-1| < 5$?

    (A) $-4 < x < 6$
    (B) $-6 < x < 6$
    (C) $x > 6$ or $x < -4$
    (D) $x > 6$ or $x < -6$

7. Which graph shows a line with a negative slope?

(A)

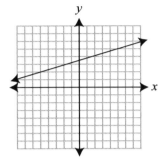

(B)

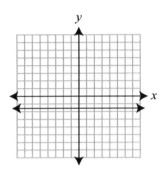

(C)

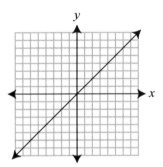

(D)

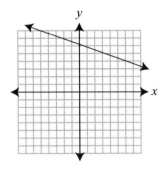

8. If $2.5(x - y + 1) = 12.5(x - .2y)$, what is the value of $x$?

(A) 0

(B) $\frac{1}{6}$

(C) $\frac{1}{5}$

(D) $\frac{1}{4}$

9. Which expression is equivalent to $(2y)^2 - x^2$?

(A) $2y^2 - 2x^2$
(B) $(2y - x)(y + x)$
(C) $(y - x)(2y + x)$
(D) $(2y - x)(2y + x)$

10. Which value is equal to $\frac{1}{9}$?

(A) $\frac{.\bar{3}}{3}$

(B) .11

(C) $\frac{1}{27} \div \frac{3}{1}$

(D) $1 - \left(\frac{2}{3}\right)^2$

11. Which of the following expressions is equal to $(4 \times 10^3) \times (3 \times 10^5)$?

(A) $1.2 \times 10^5$
(B) $1.2 \times 10^8$
(C) $1.2 \times 10^9$
(D) $1.2 \times 10^{15}$

12. 23 gymnasts competed in an event and were scored on a scale of integers. The lowest score was 4 and the highest score was 9. The table below summarizes the results.

| Score | Number of gymnasts who received that score |
|---|---|
| 4 | 2 |
| 5 | 1 |
| 6 | 8 |
| 7 | 6 |
| 8 | 5 |
| 9 | 1 |

What is the difference between the number of gymnasts who scored above the median and the number of gymnasts who scored above the mode?

(A) 2

(B) 6

(C) 8

(D) 11

13. Ms. Delgado randomly selects one of the 19 students in her class to answer a question. Later, she randomly selects one of her 19 students to answer a different question. If she selects Sienna to answer the first question, what is the probability that she selects Sienna to answer the second question also?

(A) 0

(B) $\frac{1}{18}$

(C) $\frac{1}{19}$

(D) $\frac{1}{19} \times \frac{1}{18}$

14. The figure shows two vertices of an isosceles triangle.

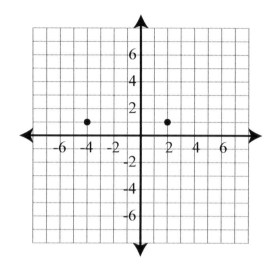

Which of the following could NOT be the third vertex of the triangle?

(A) $(-1, -5)$

(B) $(-4, 5)$

(C) $(2, -5)$

(D) $(-1, 5)$

15. Connor plays a game. On 20% of plays, he wins $3.00. On 80% of plays, he wins $5.00. What are Connor's expected winnings per play of the game?

(A) $4.00

(B) $4.20

(C) $4.60

(D) $5.00

16. Point $(a, -1)$ is on a circle with center $(5, -1)$ and radius 7. Which of the following could be the value of $a$?

   (A) 12
   (B) 7
   (C) 6
   (D) –1

17. If $n$ is an odd integer, which of the following must be an even integer?

   (A) $n^2 - 5x + 6$
   (B) $n^2 - 4n + 4$
   (C) $n^2 + 3n + 1$
   (D) $n^2 - 4n + 8$

18. Triangle ABC is shown.

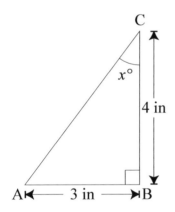

   What is the value of $\cos x°$?

   (A) $\dfrac{3}{5}$
   (B) $\dfrac{4}{5}$
   (C) $\dfrac{3}{4}$
   (D) $\dfrac{4}{3}$

19. Santiago collected data from a survey. His results are displayed in the stem-and-leaf plot shown.

| Stem | Leaf |   |   |   |   |   |
|------|------|---|---|---|---|---|
| 3    | 8    | 8 | 9 | 9 | 9 |   |
| 4    | 0    | 0 | 1 | 5 | 5 | 6 |
| 5    | 0    | 2 | 4 | 8 |   |   |
| 6    | 3    | 7 | 7 | 7 | 9 |   |
| 7    | 0    | 4 | 6 | 7 | 8 |   |

   What is the median of Santiago's data?

   (A) 52
   (B) 53
   (C) 54
   (D) 67

20. In the figure, the measures of four of the angles of a five-sided figure are shown.

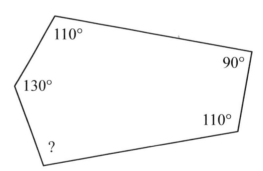

   What is the measure of the fifth angle?

   (A) 130°
   (B) 120°
   (C) 110°
   (D) 100°

21. The graph below shows the number of parking spaces available on the streets in Camila's neighborhood. The numbers on the horizontal axis represent the number parking spaces available, and the numbers on the vertical axis represent the percentage of streets with that number of parking spaces available.

Number of Parking Spaces Available on the Streets in Camila's Neighborhood

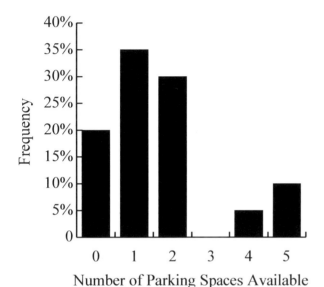

What percentage of streets have fewer than the mean number of parking spaces available?

(A) 20%
(B) 35%
(C) 55%
(D) 85%

22. In a baking mixture, the ratio of cornmeal to flour is 4:21 and the ratio of sugar to cornmeal is 15:8. If there are 14 ounces of flour in the mixture, how many ounces of sugar are there?

(A) 3
(B) 4
(C) 5
(D) 6

23. If $i^2 = -1$, which of the following is equal to $i^5$?

(A) $-i$
(B) $i$
(C) $-1$
(D) $1$

24. For what values of $x$ is it true that $\sqrt{x^2 + 1} = -|x + 1|$?

(A) 0
(B) 1
(C) all real numbers
(D) there are no real values of $x$ that make the equation true

25. Which of the following expressions represents an imaginary number?

(A) $\sqrt{\pi}$
(B) $\sqrt{2 - \pi}$
(C) $\sqrt{\pi - 2}$
(D) $2 - \sqrt{\pi}$

26. The figure below is composed of squares, regular octagons and an irregularly shaped shaded region. The area of each square is 1 in² and the area of each octagon is 7 in².

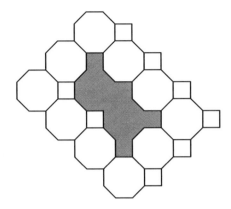

What is the area of the shaded region?

(A) 16 in²
(B) 17 in²
(C) 18 in²
(D) 19 in²

27. The figure shows 4 identical triangles on the interior of a rectangle.

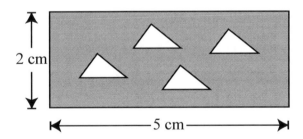

If the area of each triangle is .25 cm², what is the area of the shaded region?

(A) 9.00 cm²
(B) 9.25 cm²
(C) 9.50 cm²
(D) 9.75 cm²

28. An inequality is graphed on the number line shown.

The graph of which inequality is shown?

(A) $x \geq 2$ or $x \leq 0$
(B) $x \leq 2$ or $x \geq 0$
(C) $x \leq 2$ and $x \geq 0$
(D) $x \geq 2$ and $x \leq 0$

29. The graph shows the cost of sending a package as a function of the weight of the package.

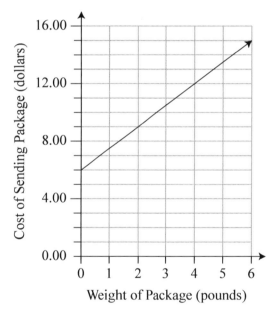

If the trend shown above continues, how much does it cost to send an 8-pound package?

(A) $17.00
(B) $17.50
(C) $18.00
(D) $18.50

30. The formula for the distance traveled by a car is $d = rt$, where $r$ is the rate at which the car is traveling and $t$ is the amount of time for which the car travels. If Car A traveled farther than Car B traveled, which of the following could be true?

    (A) Car A traveled three times as fast as Car B for half the time that Car B traveled

    (B) Car A traveled three times as fast as Car B for one third of the time that Car B traveled

    (C) Car A traveled twice as fast as Car B for half the time that Car B traveled

    (D) Car A traveled one third as fast as Car B for twice the time that Car B traveled

31. In a club there are twice as many girls as there are boys. There are 30 children in the club. How many boys must join the club in order for there to be equal numbers of boys and girls?

    (A) 30
    (B) 20
    (C) 15
    (D) 10

32. Maurice puts 4 cups of sugar and 6 cups of flour in a bowl. He mixes the components thoroughly, then removes half of the mixture and replaces it with 5 cups of pure sugar. What fraction of the mixture in the bowl at the end of this process is flour?

    (A) $\frac{1}{4}$

    (B) $\frac{3}{10}$

    (C) $\frac{7}{10}$

    (D) $\frac{3}{4}$

33. The formula for the perimeter of a rectangle is $P = 2(l + w)$, where $P$ is the perimeter and $l$ and $w$ are the length and width, respectively. If the length of Rectangle R is twice its width, which of the following expresses the perimeter of Rectangle R in terms of its width, $w$?

    (A) $3w$

    (B) $4w$

    (C) $6w$

    (D) $8w$

34. Which of the following is equivalent to $\frac{4}{1000} + 600 + \frac{7}{10} + 3$?

    (A) 603.704
    (B) 603.740
    (C) 630.704
    (D) 630.074

35. If $\begin{bmatrix} 1 & x \\ 2 & 4 \end{bmatrix} + \begin{bmatrix} 8 & 1 \\ 3 & 0 \end{bmatrix} = \begin{bmatrix} 9 & 5 \\ 5 & 4 \end{bmatrix}$, what is the value of $x$?

(A) 3
(B) 4
(C) 5
(D) 6

36. If all of Daria's friends are tall, which of the following MUST be true?

(A) Daria is tall
(B) Anyone who is not Daria's friend is not tall
(C) Everyone who is tall is Daria's friend
(D) No one who is not tall is Daria's friend

37. If $y$ is a positive number, which expression is equivalent to $y\sqrt{y^5}$?

(A) $y^6$
(B) $y^{11}$
(C) $\sqrt{y^6}$
(D) $\sqrt{y^7}$

38. Which is the most reasonable unit for measuring the mass of an adult human?

(A) kilograms
(B) grams
(C) ounces
(D) feet

39. A group of customers was asked to eat at both Restaurant A and Restaurant B and rate the service at each restaurant on a scale of 1 to 10. The box-and-whisker plot below summarizes the ratings for each restaurant.

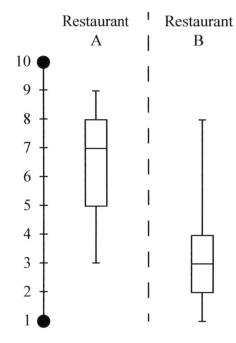

Which of the following statements is NOT true?

(A) The median rating for Restaurant A is greater than the median rating for Restaurant B.
(B) The lowest rating for Restaurant A is less than the median rating for Restaurant B.
(C) The median rating for Restaurant A is lower than the highest rating for Restaurant B.
(D) The range of ratings for Restaurant B is greater than the range of ratings for Restaurant A.

40. At night, a man who is 6 feet tall stands near a lamp post that is 9 feet tall, as shown in the figure.

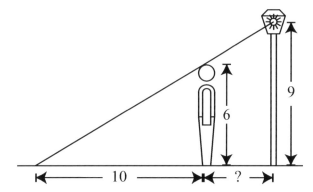

The man casts a shadow that is 10 feet long. How far is the man from the lamp post?

(A) 3 feet

(B) 4 feet

(C) 5 feet

(D) 15 feet

41. Which of the following graphs shows the solution set of $x^2 > 9$?

(A)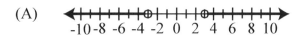

(B)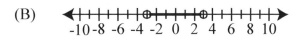

(C)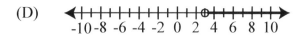

(D) ![number line](number line showing solution with open circle at 3)

42. Eliot weighs 20% less than Hector. If Eliot weighs 160 pounds, how many pounds does Hector weigh?

(A) 128

(B) 180

(C) 192

(D) 200

STOP. If there is time, you may check your work in this section only.

**STOP**

# Essay Directions

There is an essay topic printed on the next page of this test. Do not turn the page until you are told to begin. Once you are told to begin, you will have 30 minutes to write an essay on the topic provided. You may not write on another topic.

Your writing should be as clear as possible. The quality of your writing is more important than the length of your essay, but your essay should be long enough to develop your ideas and to demonstrate your writing ability.

You may plan your response in the notes section provided on the next page. Any writing you do in the notes section will NOT be counted as part of your essay. Your final draft must be written on the lined portion of your answer sheet. Only what is written on your answer sheet will be considered part of your essay. Remember that you will have only 30 minutes to plan and write your essay, so you should leave enough time to copy your final draft to the answer sheet.

Please use a blue or black pen to write your essay. Do not write outside of the box provided on the answer sheet. You may write in cursive or in print.

Please copy the following topic onto the first few lines of your answer sheet.

# Essay Topic

**Describe a situation in which you helped someone or someone helped you.**

- Do not write on any other topic.
- Write your final draft on the answer sheet, NOT in the space below.
- Write in blue or black pen.

## Notes

_____

_____

_____

_____

_____

_____

_____

_____

_____

_____

_____

_____

_____

_____

_____

_____

# ISEE
Independent School Entrance Exam

# Practice Test 4

# Answer Sheet

## Verbal Reasoning

| | | | | | |
|---|---|---|---|---|---|
| 1 ABCD | 13 ABCD | 25 ABCD |
| 2 ABCD | 14 ABCD | 26 ABCD |
| 3 ABCD | 15 ABCD | 27 ABCD |
| 4 ABCD | 16 ABCD | 28 ABCD |
| 5 ABCD | 17 ABCD | 29 ABCD |
| 6 ABCD | 18 ABCD | 30 ABCD |
| 7 ABCD | 19 ABCD | 31 ABCD |
| 8 ABCD | 20 ABCD | 32 ABCD |
| 9 ABCD | 21 ABCD | 33 ABCD |
| 10 ABCD | 22 ABCD | 34 ABCD |
| 11 ABCD | 23 ABCD | 35 ABCD |
| 12 ABCD | 24 ABCD | |

## Quantitative Reasoning

| | | | | | |
|---|---|---|---|---|---|
| 1 ABCD | 12 ABCD | 23 ABCD |
| 2 ABCD | 13 ABCD | 24 ABCD |
| 3 ABCD | 14 ABCD | 25 ABCD |
| 4 ABCD | 15 ABCD | 26 ABCD |
| 5 ABCD | 16 ABCD | 27 ABCD |
| 6 ABCD | 17 ABCD | 28 ABCD |
| 7 ABCD | 18 ABCD | 29 ABCD |
| 8 ABCD | 19 ABCD | 30 ABCD |
| 9 ABCD | 20 ABCD | 31 ABCD |
| 10 ABCD | 21 ABCD | 32 ABCD |
| 11 ABCD | 22 ABCD | |

## Reading Comprehension

| | | | | | |
|---|---|---|---|---|---|
| 1 ABCD | 11 ABCD | 21 ABCD |
| 2 ABCD | 12 ABCD | 22 ABCD |
| 3 ABCD | 13 ABCD | 23 ABCD |
| 4 ABCD | 14 ABCD | 24 ABCD |
| 5 ABCD | 15 ABCD | 25 ABCD |
| 6 ABCD | 16 ABCD | 26 ABCD |
| 7 ABCD | 17 ABCD | 27 ABCD |
| 8 ABCD | 18 ABCD | 28 ABCD |
| 9 ABCD | 19 ABCD | 29 ABCD |
| 10 ABCD | 20 ABCD | 30 ABCD |

## Mathematics Achievement

| | | | | | |
|---|---|---|---|---|---|
| 1 ABCD | 15 ABCD | 29 ABCD |
| 2 ABCD | 16 ABCD | 30 ABCD |
| 3 ABCD | 17 ABCD | 31 ABCD |
| 4 ABCD | 18 ABCD | 32 ABCD |
| 5 ABCD | 19 ABCD | 33 ABCD |
| 6 ABCD | 20 ABCD | 34 ABCD |
| 7 ABCD | 21 ABCD | 35 ABCD |
| 8 ABCD | 22 ABCD | 36 ABCD |
| 9 ABCD | 23 ABCD | 37 ABCD |
| 10 ABCD | 24 ABCD | 38 ABCD |
| 11 ABCD | 25 ABCD | 39 ABCD |
| 12 ABCD | 26 ABCD | 40 ABCD |
| 13 ABCD | 27 ABCD | 41 ABCD |
| 14 ABCD | 28 ABCD | 42 ABCD |

# Answer Sheet - Essay

Write your response in blue or black pen.

STUDENT NAME _____

| Write your essay topic here. |
| --- |
| _____ |
| _____ |
| _____ |

Write your response here.

_____

_____

_____

_____

_____

_____

_____

_____

_____

_____

_____

_____

_____

_____

_____

_____

_____

_____

_____

_____

_____

_____

_____

_____

_____

_____

_____

_____

(Answer Sheet - Essay continued)

# ISEE
Independent School Entrance Exam

# Upper Level
# Verbal Reasoning

# Practice Test 4

*This page intentionally left blank.*

# Section 1
# Verbal Reasoning

| 35 Questions | Time: 17.5 minutes |
|---|---|

This section is divided into two parts that contain two different types of questions. As soon as you have completed Part One, answer the questions in Part Two. You may write in your test booklet. For each answer you select, fill in the corresponding circle on your answer document.

## Part One — Synonyms

Each question in Part One consists of a word in capital letters followed by four answer choices. Select the one word that is most nearly the same in meaning as the word in capital letters.

SAMPLE QUESTION:                                    SAMPLE ANSWER:

    EXTEND:                                         Ⓐ ● Ⓒ Ⓓ

    (A) avoid
    (B) lengthen
    (C) criticize
    (D) discover

## Part Two — Sentence Completion

Each question in Part Two is made up of a sentence with one or two blanks. One blank indicates that one word is missing. Two blanks indicate that two words are missing. Each sentence is followed by four answer choices. Select the one word or pair of words that best completes the meaning of the sentence as a whole.

SAMPLE QUESTIONS:                                   SAMPLE ANSWERS:

    Unlike her older brother, who always acted --------,        ● Ⓑ Ⓒ Ⓓ
    Cheryl preferred to take her time.

    (A) quickly
    (B) carefully
    (C) stupidly
    (D) wisely

    Whitewater rafting is both ------- and dangerous: rapids     Ⓐ Ⓑ Ⓒ ●
    may provide thrills, but they also threaten a rafter's ------.

    (A) ancient...pride
    (B) understandable...judgment
    (C) informative...freedom
    (D) exciting...safety

STOP. Do not go on
until told to do so.

**STOP**

## Part One — Synonyms

**Directions:** Select the word that is most nearly the same in meaning as the word in capital letters.

1. COMPILE:

   (A) assemble
   (B) fill
   (C) restore
   (D) improve

2. VETO:

   (A) design
   (B) write
   (C) forbid
   (D) consider

3. HARDY:

   (A) strong
   (B) difficult
   (C) delicate
   (D) free

4. RECEPTACLE:

   (A) ghost
   (B) container
   (C) parade
   (D) chain

5. ACKNOWLEDGE:

   (A) forget
   (B) investigate
   (C) recognize
   (D) seek

6. REINFORCE:

   (A) punish
   (B) support
   (C) install
   (D) redeem

7. ADAPT:

   (A) arrange
   (B) consume
   (C) relieve
   (D) adjust

8. ERRONEOUS:

   (A) linear
   (B) logical
   (C) moderate
   (D) mistaken

9. IMPEDIMENT:

   (A) avenue
   (B) obstacle
   (C) soil
   (D) plantation

10. ARCHAIC:

   (A) ancient
   (B) circular
   (C) structural
   (D) puzzling

11. ESCORT:

    (A)    imprison
    (B)    tackle
    (C)    prosecute
    (D)    accompany

12. PROPENSITY:

    (A)    quickness
    (B)    attitude
    (C)    pride
    (D)    tendency

13. HAMPER:

    (A)    clean
    (B)    interfere
    (C)    edit
    (D)    subtract

14. HAUGHTY:

    (A)    disobedient
    (B)    stimulating
    (C)    courteous
    (D)    arrogant

15. AVID:

    (A)    enthusiastic
    (B)    indecisive
    (C)    delinquent
    (D)    prepared

16. CLAMOR:

    (A)    immigrant
    (B)    loss
    (C)    uproar
    (D)    seizure

17. SURFEIT:

    (A)    shoreline
    (B)    resignation
    (C)    excess
    (D)    agreement

## Part Two — Sentence Completion

**Directions:** Select the word or word pair that best completes the sentence.

18. Typically shy, Marcus surprised his parents when he greeted guests at the family picnic with ------- chatter.

    (A) timid
    (B) effusive
    (C) meaningless
    (D) nervous

19. Not inclined toward risk-taking by nature, Harris was naturally ------- when faced with the prospect of diving from an airplane with only a parachute for protection.

    (A) skeptical
    (B) jubilant
    (C) generous
    (D) hasty

20. Asked whether he would retire after the 1998 season, basketball star Michael Jordan -------; he said he enjoyed playing the game but was considering other options.

    (A) equivocated
    (B) pounced
    (C) vented
    (D) persevered

21. Many female news journalists feel that they must deliver lively, animated performances on screen, imitating the ------- personalities of pioneers like Katie Couric.

    (A) subdued
    (B) carefree
    (C) vivacious
    (D) visionary

22. Once close partners, technology companies Apple and Google have become bitter ------- in the struggle for dominance over smartphones and tablets.

    (A) adversaries
    (B) confidantes
    (C) allies
    (D) associates

23. Defenses at the fort were so ------- that the advancing army was able to penetrate the structure at multiple points simultaneously.

    (A) sturdy
    (B) porous
    (C) stodgy
    (D) regal

24. Among the most prized manuscripts in Yale University's collection of rare books, *Arthurian Romances* is a thick ------- written in elegant gothic script.

   (A) plot
   (B) panel
   (C) tome
   (D) faction

25. The rate of ------- is considerably higher in the United States than in other developed countries, and critics point to high U.S. prison populations as a drain on federal revenue.

   (A) intolerance
   (B) misconduct
   (C) negligence
   (D) incarceration

26. It is the responsibility of sheep-dogs to herd ------- sheep back into the flock.

   (A) obedient
   (B) unhealthy
   (C) wayward
   (D) somber

27. After a period spent wrapped in a chrysalis, caterpillars ------- from their encasements as butterflies.

   (A) descend
   (B) arrive
   (C) emerge
   (D) retreat

28. Online educator Salman Khan is known both for his ------- explanations of topics in science and mathematics and for the free access he provides to these exceptionally clear -------.

   (A) puzzling...descriptions
   (B) engaging...disciplines
   (C) rambling...proposals
   (D) lucid...tutorials

29. The life of mathematician Evariste Galois was ------- but -------: he died in a duel at an early age, but he made lasting contributions to the field of algebra.

   (A) violent...short
   (B) brief...significant
   (C) tragic...trivial
   (D) undisciplined...creative

30. The apparent ------- of Steve Martin's manic stand-up routines was an illusion; each segment of every act was carefully -------, even the seemingly improvised moments.

   (A) wizardry...restrained
   (B) ease...promoted
   (C) spontaneity...planned
   (D) order...staged

31. The ------- of tennis player Patrick Rafter was -------; he attained the top ranking in the world on July 26th, 1999 and lost it only a week later, never to reclaim it.

   (A) dedication...worthwhile
   (B) dominance...fleeting
   (C) authority...prolonged
   (D) ambition...thwarted

32. Because it was necessary to ------- Kevin's blood cholesterol levels on a regular basis, his doctor ordered him to come the clinic for ------- testing.

    (A) demote...cumbersome
    (B) enhance...costly
    (C) salvage...interminable
    (D) monitor...periodic

33. There is a ------- between a nation, which is a group of people, and a -------, which is a political authority.

    (A) similarity...race
    (B) distinction...state
    (C) uniformity...fellowship
    (D) competition...government

34. Jisheng Han's scientific research gave ------- to claims that acupuncture could relieve pain; doctors had previously dismissed such claims as -------.

    (A) credibility...unfounded
    (B) traction...plausible
    (C) license...inactive
    (D) comfort...reputable

35. Carlos had been warned that his new room would be -------, but upon arrival, he found the space to be even more ------- than he had expected.

    (A) dingy...solitary
    (B) remote...vacant
    (C) extensive...peculiar
    (D) compact ... cramped

STOP. Do not go on until told to do so. **STOP**

# ISEE
Independent School Entrance Exam

# Upper Level
# Quantitative Reasoning

# Practice Test 4

# Section 2
# Quantitative Reasoning

This section has two parts that contain two different kinds of questions. Do not pause after Part One. Continue working through Part Two. You may write in your test booklet.

Letters such as $x$ and $y$ stand for real numbers. All figures are drawn to scale unless otherwise stated.

**Part One — Word Problems**

Each question in Part One consists of a word problem followed by four answer choices. Select the best answer from the four choices given and fill in the corresponding circle on your answer document.

---

EXAMPLE 1:                                        SAMPLE ANSWER

Ⓐ Ⓑ Ⓒ ●

Which of the following fractions is greater than $\frac{3}{4}$?

(A) $\frac{1}{5}$

(B) $\frac{1}{4}$

(C) $\frac{2}{5}$

(D) $\frac{4}{5}$

The correct answer is $\frac{4}{5}$, so circle D is darkened.

---

*Go on to the next page.* ➡

# QR

**Part Two — Quantitative Comparisons**

In Part Two, use the given information to compare the quantities given in Column A and Column B. Choose one of these four answer choices:

(A) The quantity in Column A is greater.
(B) The quantity in Column B is greater.
(C) The two quantities are equal.
(D) The relationship cannot be determined from the information given.

---

EXAMPLE 2:

SAMPLE ANSWER

Ⓐ Ⓑ ● Ⓓ

| Column A | Column B |
|----------|----------|
| The greatest integer that is less than 4.1 | The smallest integer that is greater than 3.9 |

The quantity in Column A (4) is the same as the quantity in Column B (4), so circle C is darkened.

---

EXAMPLE 3:

SAMPLE ANSWER

Ⓐ Ⓑ Ⓒ ●

$$x^2 > 4$$

| Column A | Column B |
|----------|----------|
| $x$ | 2 |

One possible value for $x$ is 3 because $3^2 = 9$ and $9 > 4$. Another possible value for $x$ is $-3$ because $(-3)^2 = 9$ also. Because the quantity in Column A (3 or $-3$, for instance) may be greater than or less than the quantity in Column B (2), the relationship cannot be determined and circle D is darkened.

STOP. Do not go on until told to do so.

## Part One — Word Problems

**Directions:** Choose the best answer from the four choices given.

1. Let $x$ and $y$ be defined as follows:

$$x = (-20) + (-18) + (-16) + \cdots + 16 + 18$$
$$y = (-19) + (-17) + (-15) + \cdots + 19 + 21$$

What is the value of $x + y$?

(A) $-20$
(B) $0$
(C) $1$
(D) $21$

2. If $(x+3)(x+k) = x^2 + 10x + 21$ for all values of $x$, what is the value of $k$?

(A) $2$
(B) $3$
(C) $5$
(D) $7$

3. The volume of a box is given by the formula $V = lwh$, where $l, w,$ and $h$ are the length, width and height of the box, respectively. If the length and width of the box are decreased by 60% each and the height of the box is increased by 50%, what is the percent decrease in the volume of the box?

(A) $76\%$
(B) $70\%$
(C) $38\%$
(D) $10\%$

4. Triangle XYZ is similar to triangle RST.

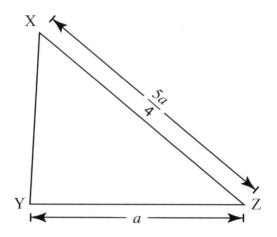

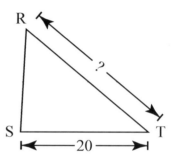

What is the length of $\overline{RT}$?

(A) $20a$
(B) $25a$
(C) $16$
(D) $25$

5. If $x$ is a multiple of 45 and $y$ is a multiple of 105, what is the largest value that must be a factor of $x + y$?

   (A) 105
   (B) 15
   (C) 5
   (D) 3

6. The heights of a class of 20 students are measured while the students are in 3$^{rd}$ grade and then measured again when the students are in 8$^{th}$ grade. The mean height of students in the class increases by 6 inches from 3$^{rd}$ grade to 8$^{th}$ grade. Which of the following statements must be true about the changes in the class from 3$^{rd}$ grade to 8$^{th}$ grade?

   (A) Each student in the class grew by 6 inches
   (B) The sum of the students' heights increased by 6 inches
   (C) The sum of the students' heights increased by 120 inches
   (D) Some of the students grew more than other students

7. What is the value of the following expression?
$$\frac{49^2}{3 \times 7^3}$$

   (A) $\frac{7}{3}$

   (B) $\frac{3}{7}$

   (C) $\frac{1}{7}$

   (D) $\frac{1}{21}$

8. A tank that originally contains 50 liters of water is drained at a constant rate of 5 liters of water per minute until it is empty. Which of the following graphs best represents what happens to the volume of the water in the tank over time?

   (A)

   (B)

   (C)

   (D)

9.  The average ages of family members in 4 households are listed below, along with the number of family members in each household. What is the mean age of all 20 people in the 4 households?

| Household | Mean Age (years) | Number of family members |
|-----------|------------------|--------------------------|
| A | 10 | 8 |
| B | 20 | 5 |
| C | 25 | 4 |
| D | 40 | 3 |

(A)  17.5 years
(B)  20.0 years
(C)  22.5 years
(D)  25.0 years

10.  If $de = 2d + 2e$, which of the following is an expression for $d$ in terms of $e$?

(A)  $\dfrac{2e}{e-2}$

(B)  $\dfrac{e}{e-1}$

(C)  $e-1$

(D)  $e-2$

11.  Let $p \lozenge q = p^2 - q^2$ for all real numbers $p$ and $q$. Which of the following is equivalent to $4 \lozenge x$?

(A)  $(4-x)^2$
(B)  $(4-x)(4+x)$
(C)  $-(16+x^2)$
(D)  $x^2 - 16$

12.  Landry surveyed a class of 20 students to determine how many bowls of cereal each student had eaten in the past week. He correctly determined that the mode of his data was 4, the range was 6, and the median was 2. He then graphed his results on the bar chart below, but he made one or more mistakes in creating the graph.

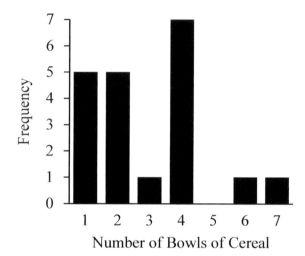

Which of the three statistical measures Landry calculated is misrepresented by the graph?

(A)  The mode
(B)  The range
(C)  The median
(D)  The range and the median

13.  The lengths of the sides of a rectangle are measured in whole centimeters, and the perimeter of the rectangle is 18 cm. What is the greatest possible area of the rectangle?

(A)  14 cm²
(B)  18 cm²
(C)  20 cm²
(D)  81 cm²

14. The graph shows the revenue in dollars for selling cupcakes at a bake sale as a function of the number of cupcakes sold.

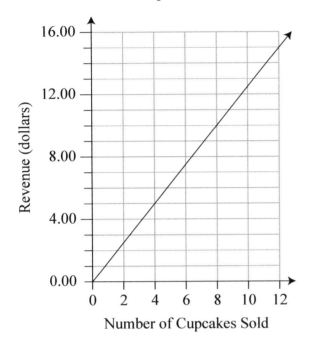

How much money was each cupcake sold for, in dollars?

(A) $1.00
(B) $1.25
(C) $1.30
(D) $1.50

15. Clock A chimes once every $x$ minutes. Clock B chimes once every $y$ minutes. Both clocks chime at midnight. Which of the following quantities, if known, could be used to determine the first time at which the clocks chime together after midnight?

(A) $x$
(B) $y$
(C) The greatest common factor of $x$ and $y$
(D) The least common multiple of $x$ and $y$

16. Edith records the number of points scored by the five players on a basketball team during a game. If two players score the same number of points and one player scores more than half of the points, which of the following circle graphs could represent the number of points scored by the team?

(A)

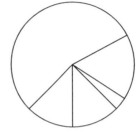

(B)

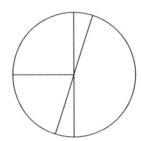

(C)

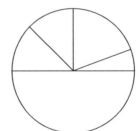

(D)

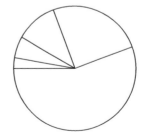

17. The figure shows a triangular pyramid with arrows drawn on the faces shown. The faces that are not shown are marked with the symbol X.

Which of the following could be a net of the triangular pyramid?

(A) 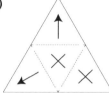     (B) 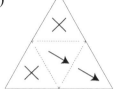     (C) 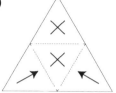     (D)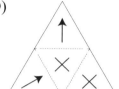

18. Quinn made a scale drawing of her street that includes her home, the post office, her school, and the library, as shown below.

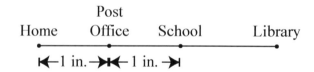

Quinn's home is 6 kilometers from the school, and the school is 4 kilometers from the library. On the scale drawing, how many inches from the post office is the library?

(A) $1\frac{1}{3}$ inches

(B) $1\frac{2}{3}$ inches

(C) 2 inches

(D) $2\frac{1}{3}$ inches

# QR

## Part Two—Quantitative Comparisons

**Directions:** Using the information given in each question, compare the quantity in Column A to the quantity in Column B. All questions in Part Two have these answer choices:

(A)   The quantity in Column A is greater.
(B)   The quantity in Column B is greater.
(C)   The two quantities are equal.
(D)   The relationship cannot be determined from the information given.

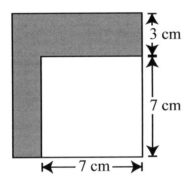

The figure shows a square within a larger rectangle. The perimeter of the larger rectangle is 38 cm.

| Column A | Column B |
|----------|----------|
| 19.  The area of the square | The area of the shaded region |

$s < 0$

| Column A | Column B |
|----------|----------|
| 20.      $\dfrac{1}{s}$ | $|s| + s$ |

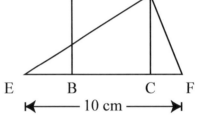

ABCD is a square whose perimeter is 20 centimeters.

| Column A | Column B |
|----------|----------|
| 21.  The area of square ABCD | The area of triangle DEF |

$w, x, y,$ and $z$ are four consecutive integers.

| Column A | Column B |
|----------|----------|
| 22.      $w + x + y + z$ | $w \times x \times y \times z$ |

**Answer choices for all questions on this page:**

(A) The quantity in Column A is greater.
(B) The quantity in Column B is greater.
(C) The two quantities are equal.
(D) The relationship cannot be determined from the information given.

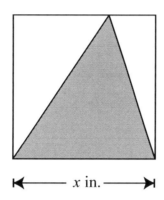

|← —— $x$ in. ——→|

The figure shows a triangle inscribed in a square.

| Column A | Column B |
|---|---|
| 23. The area of the shaded region | $\dfrac{x^2}{3}$ inches² |

---

Line $l$ is perpendicular to line $k$. Line $k$ passes through the point $(4, 6)$ and line $l$ passes through the point $(-1, 3)$.

| Column A | Column B |
|---|---|
| 24. The slope of line $l$ | The slope of line $k$ |

---

| Column A | Column B |
|---|---|
| 25. $2 \times (3 - 5) \times (9 + 1)$ | $(6 - 8) \times 10 \times (13 - 11)$ |

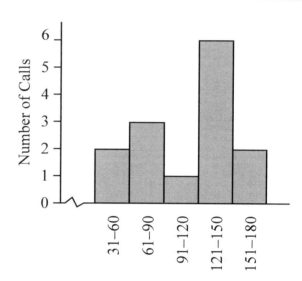

Length of Call (seconds)

The histogram above shows the lengths of some telephone calls.

| Column A | Column B |
|---|---|
| 26. The shortest call length | The difference between the median call length and the longest call length |

# QR

**Answer choices for all questions on this page:**

(A) The quantity in Column A is greater.
(B) The quantity in Column B is greater.
(C) The two quantities are equal.
(D) The relationship cannot be determined from the information given.

---

There are 4 identical blue marbles in a jar and 6 identical red marbles. Each blue marble weighs 3 ounces more than each red marble. The blue marbles weigh 32 ounces all together.

| Column A | Column B |
|----------|----------|
| 27.  32 ounces | The combined weight of the 6 red marbles |

---

The number of occupied apartments in a building increased by 50% from February to March. The number of occupied apartments then decreased from March to April, and fewer apartments were occupied in April than were occupied in February.

| Column A | Column B |
|----------|----------|
| 28. The percent decrease in the number of occupied apartments from March to April | 50% |

---

| Column A | Column B |
|----------|----------|
| 29.  $(a^2 - b^2)(a+b)$ | $(a+b)^2(a-b)$ |

---

Town A lies 9 miles directly south of Town B. Town C lies 12 miles directly east of Town B.

| Column A | Column B |
|----------|----------|
| 30. The shortest distance from Town A to Town C | 21 miles |

---

$$a \neq b$$

| Column A | Column B |
|----------|----------|
| 31.  $2 \times (a-b)^2$ | $a^2 - 2ab + b^2$ |

---

Jim has 6 coins in his pocket: 4 dimes and 2 nickels. He pulls 3 of the coins out of his pocket at random.

| Column A | Column B |
|----------|----------|
| 32. The probability that all three coins are dimes | $\frac{1}{5}$ |

**STOP.** If there is time, you may check your work in this section only.  **STOP**

*This page intentionally left blank.*

# ISEE

Independent School Entrance Exam

# Upper Level
# Reading Comprehension

# Practice Test 4

*This page intentionally left blank.*

# Section 3
# Reading Comprehension

This section contains five short reading passages. Each passage is followed by six questions based on its content. Answer the questions following each passage on the basis of what is stated or implied in that passage. You may write in your test booklet.

Questions 1–6

1     As recently as 1970, one could visit the
2  Koh Ker temple complex in northwestern
3  Cambodia and find among the beautiful ruins
4  two statues, known as the Kneeling Attendants,
5  that had stood at the site for over a thousand
6  years. Today, a visit to the same site will
7  reward travelers with a view of only the broken
8  bases of the statues. To see the Kneeling
9  Attendants themselves, one must instead visit
10  the Metropolitan Museum of Art in New York
11  City. This is a sad situation, both for foreign
12  sightseers who would prefer to find the statues
13  in their original context and for Cambodians
14  whose cultural legacy the statues represent.
15     The Kneeling Attendants are just one
16  example of a damaging trend in which important
17  cultural artifacts are illegally removed from
18  their proper homes and displayed in distant,
19  sterile museums. The museums benefit greatly
20  from the arrangement: exotic treasures from
21  distant lands sell admission tickets. But recent
22  negative publicity surrounding such artifacts has

23  begun to damage the museums' reputations, and
24  museum administrators are debating what to do.
25     What would ever convince a well-meaning
26  museum curator to accept such treasures in the
27  first place? Curators are, after all, historians of
28  art and culture, and they often care deeply for
29  the communities they study. What rationale
30  might they give for taking advantage of illegal
31  looting?
32     One reason is that such pieces are often
33  taken from their homelands during periods of
34  national conflict that threatens these priceless
35  works with destruction. Many great pieces
36  of architecture and art have been damaged or
37  destroyed in war. Cambodia suffered a period
38  of terrible violence in the 1970's, and had the
39  Kneeling Attendants not been removed, they
40  may not have survived the conflict. But now,
41  decades later, Cambodia is a stable democracy.
42  Western museums must acknowledge this fact
43  and return the art that was taken.

1. The author's primary claim is that

   (A) war may damage priceless art
   (B) museums focus too much on ticket sales
   (C) artifacts should be returned to their proper homes
   (D) negative publicity is bad for museums

2. In line 13, the phrase "original context" refers to

   (A) a Cambodian museum
   (B) an event that occurred over a thousand years ago
   (C) the Metropolitan Museum of Art
   (D) the Koh Ker temple complex

3. The passage implies that the author believes

   (A) all foreign artifacts in western museums were taken illegally
   (B) conflict doesn't threaten artifacts in Cambodia today
   (C) museum administrators don't know where their art comes from
   (D) more sightseers visit New York City than visit Cambodia

4. The questions in the third paragraph (lines 25-31) serve to

   (A) challenge an assumption
   (B) highlight an apparent contradiction
   (C) dramatize the author's confusion
   (D) identify a misunderstanding

5. The author mentions that the 1970's were a violent period for Cambodia in order to

   (A) suggest a justification for removal of artifacts
   (B) mourn the victims of violence
   (C) account for recent damage to the Kneeling Attendants
   (D) praise Cambodia's progress toward democracy

6. The author describes the Kneeling Attendants as all of the following EXCEPT

   (A) cultural artifacts
   (B) exotic treasures
   (C) priceless works
   (D) fragile antiques

Questions 7–12

1     Don't let the name fool you: a black hole is
2 anything but empty space. Rather, it is a great
3 amount of matter packed into a very small area
4 —think of a star ten times more massive than
5 the Sun squeezed into a sphere approximately
6 the diameter of New York City. The result is a
7 gravitational field so strong that nothing, not
8 even light, can escape. In recent years, NASA
9 instruments have painted a new picture of these
10 strange objects that are, to many, the most
11 fascinating objects in space.
12     Although the term "black hole" was not
13 coined until 1967 by Princeton physicist John
14 Wheeler, scientists have long speculated about
15 an object in space so massive and dense that
16 light could not escape it. Most famously, black
17 holes were predicted by Einstein's theory of
18 general relativity, which showed that when
19 a massive star dies, it leaves behind a small,
20 dense remnant core. If the core's mass is more
21 than about three times the mass of the Sun,
22 the equations showed, the force of gravity
23 overwhelms all other forces and produces a
24 black hole.
25     Scientists can't directly observe black
26 holes with telescopes, which can only detect
27 x-rays, light, or other forms of electromagnetic
28 radiation. They can, however, infer the presence
29 of black holes by detecting their effects on other

30 matter nearby. If a black hole passes through
31 a cloud of interstellar matter, for example, it
32 will draw matter inward in a process known
33 as accretion. A similar process can occur if
34 a normal star passes close to a black hole. In
35 this case, the attractive force of the black hole
36 can tear the star apart. As the attracted matter
37 accelerates and heats up, it emits x-rays that
38 radiate into space. Recent discoveries offer
39 some tantalizing evidence that black holes have
40 a dramatic influence on the neighborhoods
41 around them—emitting powerful bursts of
42 radiation, devouring nearby stars, and spurring
43 the growth of new stars in some areas while
44 stalling it in others.
45     Most black holes form from the remnants of
46 a large star that dies in a supernova explosion.
47 Scientists theorize, though, that the largest black
48 holes result from stellar collisions. Soon after
49 its launch in December 2004, NASA's Swift
50 telescope observed powerful, fleeting flashes
51 of light known as gamma ray bursts. NASA's
52 Hubble Space Telescope later collected data
53 from the "afterglow," of these bursts, and
54 together the observations led astronomers
55 to speculate that a star and a black hole had
56 collided, producing a powerful explosion and
57 another black hole.

7.  In the first paragraph, the author gives New York City as an example of something that is

    (A) relatively small
    (B) very dense
    (C) exceptionally large
    (D) comparatively empty

8.  The passage states that which of the following events would cause x-rays to be released?

    (A) two stars colliding
    (B) a star dying
    (C) matter accelerating
    (D) a new star growing

9.  Which property is most important in determining whether a dying star becomes a black hole?

    (A) volume
    (B) area
    (C) brightness
    (D) mass

10. The "astronomers" (line 54) likely view the conclusion that "a star and a black hole had collided" (lines 55-56) as

    (A) largely unfounded
    (B) inherently contradictory
    (C) highly probable
    (D) absolutely certain

11. The passage suggests that scientists might locate a black hole by

    (A) studying neighboring matter
    (B) seeing it with a telescope
    (C) solving the equations of relativity
    (D) looking for dark spaces in the sky

12. In line 42, "spurring" most nearly means

    (A) exploring
    (B) hindering
    (C) undermining
    (D) stimulating

1     Ona was an excellent cook. She always
2  had something brewing when company was
3  expected, and visitors to her and Baba's house
4  were greeted upon entering with the smell of
5  garlic roasting or onions frying or bread baking.
6  So it came as a surprise when, on a Saturday
7  afternoon in February, my parents and I arrived
8  for a visit to find the house smelling of nothing
9  in particular.
10     Ona, gracious in her own defense, offered
11  my parents a warm but confused greeting at the
12  door. "Carol! David! So nice to have you! If
13  only I had known you were coming, I would
14  have had something in the oven. I hope you
15  don't mind the mess!"
16     As Ona turned slowly to lead us inside, my
17  father turned to my mother with a furrowed
18  brow and whispered, "Two o'clock, right?" My
19  mother nodded. My father looked at his watch,
20  then back to my mother indignantly, raising the
21  watch face so that she could see the time. The
22  hour hand was exactly at two.
23     Their muted exchange was interrupted by

24  Ona's voice from the foyer. "Come in then, but
25  don't bring the cold with you!" She laughed.
26     We entered, brushing the snow from our
27  coats and stomping our boots on the mat. My
28  mother helped me out of my many winter
29  zippers and buttons while my father greeted
30  Baba with a hug and a smile. Eva the cat
31  brushed between my ankles on her way to the
32  door, which Ona closed just in time. "That's
33  what they're good for I suppose," she said.
34  "Keeping the winter out and the animals in."
35     "Mom," my mother said, turning to Ona,
36  "did we get it wrong on the phone the other
37  day? I thought we decided to come this weekend
38  instead of next weekend because of Alice's
39  flute recital." I tensed at the mention of my
40  upcoming performance.
41     Ona gazed at my mother blankly, half
42  smiling out of habit, but her mind was at
43  work processing my mother's words. She
44  said nothing. It was only later that we would
45  discover she had no recollection of the phone
46  call at all.

13. The narrator of the passage is named

    (A) David
    (B) Carol
    (C) Alice
    (D) Eva

14. Which of the following statements about family relationships is directly supported by the passage?

    (A) The narrator's mother is Ona's daughter
    (B) The narrator's father is Ona's son
    (C) The narrator's mother is Baba's daughter
    (D) The narrator's father is Baba's son

15. The passage is primarily focused on

    (A) Ona's gracious hospitality
    (B) a failure of memory that leads to confusion
    (C) the importance of planning in advance
    (D) the value of a warm home on a cold day

16. Why is it significant that the house smells of nothing in particular when the narrator and her parents arrive?

    (A) It suggests that Ona is not expecting a visit.
    (B) It shows that Ona is not genuinely happy to see them.
    (C) It reveals that Ona has lost her desire to cook.
    (D) It implies that Ona was too busy cleaning to cook anything.

17. The narrator's father shows the narrator's mother his watch (lines 19-21) in order to

    (A) scold her for not informing Ona of their impending visit
    (B) support his belief that the family arrived on time
    (C) note the time the visit begins
    (D) express irritation that the watch isn't working

18. As used in line 23, the word "exchange" most nearly means

    (A) swap
    (B) substitution
    (C) interaction
    (D) stillness

Questions 19–24

1     As the country turns its eyes to Washington,
2 D.C. to witness the inauguration of a new
3 President, it is worth a moment to reflect on the
4 geology that helps make our capital the most
5 impressive city in the United States. The history
6 of Washington revolves around stone. All of the
7 most iconic landmarks in our nation's capital—
8 from the U.S. Capitol to the Washington
9 Monument—have a rich geological history.
10     The two most recognizable landmarks,
11 the White House and the U.S. Capitol, are
12 both made of the same material: Aquia
13 Creek sandstone. This stone, also known as
14 "freestone," was a popular building material
15 in the late 18$^{th}$ and early 19$^{th}$ centuries. George
16 Washington personally selected it as the
17 building stone for many early government
18 buildings. At the government's request, the
19 architect Pierre L'Enfant purchased a quarry
20 of this stone in 1791 about 40 miles south of
21 Washington. Much of this quarry's stone, which
22 was deposited during the Early Cretaceous
23 period (between 100 and 140 million years
24 ago), was used in the construction of D.C.'s
25 most famous government buildings, including
26 the White House, the U.S. Capitol and the U.S.
27 Treasury.
28     But the Aquia Creek sandstone didn't hold
29 up to weathering processes very well. After
30 British troops ransacked the city in 1814 and
31 burned the White House and the U.S. Capitol,
32 the walls of the White House had visible cracks.

33 Despite attempts to cover up the damage with
34 whitewash, it became apparent to architects
35 of the day that they should avoid Aquia Creek
36 sandstone in constructing future buildings. The
37 last known use of Aquia Creek sandstone was in
38 several gate houses built near the U.S. Capitol,
39 most recently in 1827.
40     The demise of Aquia Creek construction
41 ushered in the "brownstone" era of the mid-19$^{th}$
42 century, when Washington architects favored
43 Red Seneca sandstone. More resilient than
44 Aquia Creek sandstone, Red Seneca sandstone
45 can withstand adverse weather conditions.
46 Deposited during the Triassic period more than
47 200 million years ago, it comes in a range of
48 colors from reddish-brown to a deeper purplish-
49 brown; the stone attains a darker hue after it is
50 quarried and exposed to the air.
51     Red Seneca's name comes from the location
52 of the quarry that supplied the stone, about
53 20 miles from D.C. at the confluence of the
54 Potomac River and Seneca Creek. Sandstone
55 from this quarry was used to construct the
56 main building of the Smithsonian Institution,
57 also known as the "Castle." The Castle was
58 originally a lilac-gray color, but after years of
59 oxidation the sandstone altered to a dark red.
60 A similar oxidation process affected the U.S.
61 Capitol Rotunda and the floors of the U.S.
62 Capitol, all of which were built from the same
63 Red Seneca sandstone during the brownstone
64 era.

19. The primary purpose of the passage is to

    (A) announce the inauguration of a new president
    (B) detail the process of building with sandstone
    (C) criticize George Washington's choice of construction materials
    (D) explore the geology behind a city's buildings

20. The fourth paragraph (lines 40-50) suggests that the Smithsonian was constructed with Red Seneca sandstone because of the stone's

    (A) durability
    (B) varying colors
    (C) abundance
    (D) low cost

21. Which of the following attributes of Aquia Creek sandstone is NOT indicated in the passage?

    (A) where it was quarried
    (B) when it was last used in Washington
    (C) what color it is
    (D) why it is no longer used

22. According the passage, what causes Red Seneca sandstone to turn red?

    (A) adverse weather conditions
    (B) oxidation
    (C) the quarrying process
    (D) long periods underground

23. Which of the following describes the organization of the passage?

    (A) The past is contrasted with the present
    (B) The reasons for a decision are explored
    (C) A context is mentioned, then details are stated
    (D) Both sides of a controversy are considered

24. According to the passage, which of the following could NOT have been built after 1827?

    (A) The Smithsonian Castle
    (B) The U.S. Capitol Rotunda
    (C) The Washington Monument
    (D) The U.S. Treasury

Questions 25–30

1     I returned from the City about three o'clock
2 on that May afternoon pretty well disgusted with
3 life. I had been three months in the Old Country
4 and was fed up with it. If anyone had told me a
5 year ago that I would have been feeling like that
6 I should have laughed at him; but there was the
7 fact. The weather made me liverish, the talk of
8 the ordinary Englishman made me sick, and the
9 amusements of London seemed as flat as soda-
10 water that has been standing in the sun. 'Richard
11 Hannay,' I kept telling myself, 'you have got
12 into the wrong ditch, my friend, and you had
13 better climb out.'
14     It made me bite my lips to think of the plans
15 I had been building up those last years in South
16 Africa. I had got my pile—not one of the big
17 ones, but good enough for me; and I had figured
18 out all kinds of ways of enjoying myself. My
19 father had brought me out from Scotland at the
20 age of six, and I had never been home since; so
21 England was a sort of Arabian Nights to me, and

22 I counted on stopping there for the rest of my
23 days.
24     But from the first I was disappointed with
25 it. In about a week I was tired of seeing sights,
26 and in less than a month I had had enough of
27 restaurants and theatres and race-meetings.
28 I had no real pal to go about with, which
29 probably explains things. Plenty of people
30 invited me to their houses, but they didn't seem
31 much interested in me. They would fling me a
32 question or two about South Africa, and then
33 get on their own affairs. A lot of Imperialist
34 ladies asked me to tea to meet schoolmasters
35 from New Zealand and editors from Vancouver,
36 and that was the dismalest business of all. Here
37 was I, thirty-seven years old, sound of mind
38 and limb, with enough money to have a good
39 time, yawning my head off all day. I had just
40 about settled to clear out and get back to the
41 grasslands of Africa, for I was the best bored
42 man in England—until that fateful evening.

25. At the conclusion of the passage, the narrator suggests which of the following?

    (A) He had firmly decided to leave for Africa.
    (B) Something significant happened that evening.
    (C) He was relieved to have no important obligations.
    (D) England lacked wide-open spaces.

26. In line 3, the term "Old Country" refers to

    (A) England
    (B) Vancouver
    (C) New Zealand
    (D) Africa

27. The primary purpose of the passage is to

    (A) establish that the narrator spent his early life in Scotland
    (B) explain why the narrator prefers Africa to England
    (C) criticize England for its lack of entertainment
    (D) describe the narrator's dissatisfaction with England

28. The narrator describes himself as

    (A) poor and unhappy
    (B) bored and exhausted
    (C) mentally and physically healthy
    (D) quiet and reclusive

29. The narrator mentions "soda water that has been standing in the sun" (lines 9-10) in order to

    (A) emphasize the warmth of London
    (B) give an example of an amusement found in London
    (C) draw a contrast between himself and the ordinary Englishman
    (D) make a comparison to something flavorless and unexciting

30. Prior to arriving in England, the narrator expected to

    (A) stay in England forever
    (B) visit for several months before returning to Africa
    (C) enjoy himself in England until he ran out of money
    (D) stop in England, then continue to New Zealand or Vancouver

STOP. If there is time, you may check your work on this section only.

**STOP**

*This page intentionally left blank.*

# ISEE

Independent School Entrance Exam

# Upper Level
# Mathematics Achievement

# Practice Test 4

*This page intentionally left blank.*

**4**

# Section 4
# Mathematics Achievement

Choose the best answer from the four choices given. Fill in the corresponding circle on your answer document. You may write in the test booklet.

---

SAMPLE QUESTION:                                  SAMPLE ANSWER

Ⓐ ● Ⓒ Ⓓ

What number is 40% of 50?

(A)  10
(B)  20
(C)  30
(D)  40

The correct answer is 20, so circle B is darkened.

---

STOP. Do not go on
until told to do so.

**STOP**

1. Which expression is equivalent to $(a+2)(3a+5)$?

   (A) $3a^2 + 10$
   (B) $4a + 7$
   (C) $3a^2 + 10a + 10$
   (D) $3a^2 + 11a + 10$

2. Noah recorded the number of sports played by each student in his class in the table below.

   | Number of Sports | Number of students playing that number of sports |
   | --- | --- |
   | 0 | 5 |
   | 1 | 3 |
   | 2 | 6 |
   | 3 | 7 |
   | 4 | 5 |

   What is the mode of the data?

   (A) 0
   (B) 3
   (C) 4
   (D) 5

3. $2.78 \times 10^{-1} - 6.0 \times 10^{-3} =$

   (A) $2.72 \times 10^{-1}$
   (B) $2.18 \times 10^{-2}$
   (C) $-5.9722 \times 10^{-3}$
   (D) $-2.72 \times 10^{-1}$

4. "The square of any number is greater than the original number."

   Which of the following proves that the statement above is FALSE?

   (A) $1^2 = 1$
   (B) $(-1)^2 = 1$
   (C) $2^2 = 4$
   (D) $\left(-\frac{1}{2}\right)^2 = \frac{1}{4}$

5. The figure below consists of identical equilateral triangles. The area of the shaded region is 28 in².

   What is the total area of the figure?

   (A) 32 in²
   (B) 35 in²
   (C) 36 in²
   (D) 42 in²

6. A survey of a random sample of 500 adults from Florida found that exactly 70% identified themselves as middle-class. Of the following conclusions, which is best justified by this survey?

(A) It is likely that the proportion of adults in Florida who identify as middle-class falls between 65% and 75%.

(B) It is likely that the proportion of adults in the United States who identify as middle-class falls between 65% and 75%.

(C) The proportion of adults in Florida who identify as middle-class is exactly 70%.

(D) If a different random sample of 500 adults from Florida were surveyed, exactly 70% would identify as middle-class.

7. Meredith and Leiko each have a bag of candy. Each bag contains 10 red candies and 1 green candy. If both Meredith and Leiko randomly take one candy from their respective bags, what is the probability that both candies are green?

(A) $\frac{1}{11} \times \frac{1}{10}$

(B) $\frac{1}{11} \times \frac{1}{11}$

(C) $\frac{1}{10} \times \frac{1}{10}$

(D) 1

8. If $(a+b)^2 = b(2a+b) + 9$, which of the following gives all possible values of $a$?

(A) $-3$ only

(B) $-2$ only

(C) $-3$ or $3$

(D) $-2$ or $2$

9. Each day for a week, Willis noted the number of students in his English class who were wearing jeans. He made the following bar chart but forgot to label the marks on the vertical axis with numbers.

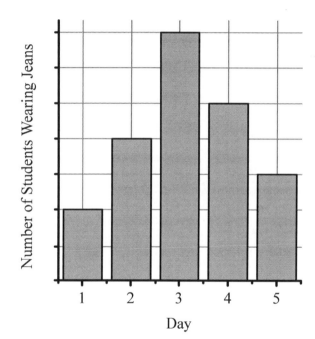

The range of Willis's data is 15. How many students were wearing jeans on Day 2?

(A) 12

(B) 15

(C) 16

(D) 20

10. For what values of $y$ is the equation $-1 = \dfrac{y-1}{1-y}$ true?

(A) $-1$ only
(B) $1$ only
(C) all real numbers except 1
(D) there are no real values of $y$ that make the equation true.

11. How many common multiples do 28 and 36 have?

(A) 2
(B) 3
(C) 4
(D) More than four

12. A restaurant offers three appetizers, four main courses, and two desserts on its menu. If a meal consists of one appetizer, one main course, and one dessert, how many different meals are possible at this restaurant?

(A) 9
(B) 18
(C) 24
(D) 27

13. The diagram shows a straight river which flows east to west. Points A, B, C and D are on the banks of the river, and point P is south of the river.

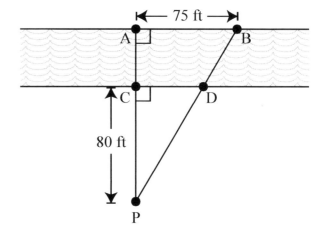

If the river is 40 feet wide, what is the distance from C to D?

(A) 25 feet
(B) 40 feet
(C) 45 feet
(D) 50 feet

14. Which gives all values of $x$ for which $|x-1|+3 < 2$?

(A) $x < 0$ or $x > 2$
(B) $x > 0$ and $x < 2$
(C) all real values of $x$
(D) there are no real values of $x$ that make the statement true.

15. What is the value of the numerical expression $5^{3+1}$?

(A) 625
(B) 130
(C) 126
(D) 125

16. If $5t(1+3t) = 15t\left(t - \dfrac{1}{t}\right)$, which of the following gives all possible values of $t$?

(A) $-3$

(B) $3$

(C) $\pm 3$

(D) $\pm\dfrac{1}{3}$

17. The average wait per person for an amusement park ride was 10 minutes on Tuesday and 15 minutes on Wednesday. If 50% more people rode the ride on Wednesday than on Tuesday, what was the average wait per person over both days?

(A) 12.0 minutes
(B) 12.5 minutes
(C) 13.0 minutes
(D) 13.5 minutes

18. While biking, Jan drinks .5 liters of water per hour. There are 3.785 liters in one gallon. Which of the following expresses the number of gallons of water Jan drinks while biking for 4 hours?

(A) $\dfrac{4}{.5 \times 3.785}$

(B) $\dfrac{4 \times 3.785}{.5}$

(C) $4 \times 3.785 \times .5$

(D) $\dfrac{4 \times .5}{3.785}$

19. An inequality is graphed on the number line shown.

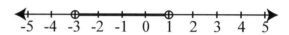

The graph of which inequality is shown?

(A) $x > 3$ or $x < 1$
(B) $x < -3$ or $x > 1$
(C) $x < -3$ and $x > 1$
(D) $x > -3$ and $x < 1$

20. Which is the most reasonable unit for measuring the volume of a beach ball?

(A) cubic feet
(B) milliliters
(C) kilograms
(D) cubic kilometers

21. The graphs of four lines are shown. Which graph shows the line with the greatest slope?

    (A)

    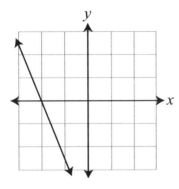

    (B)

    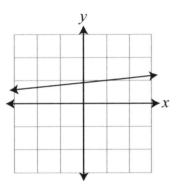

    (C)

    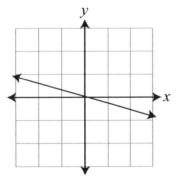

    (D)

    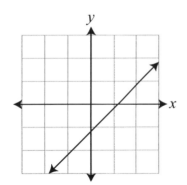

22. A basket contains peanuts, walnuts and pine nuts. The ratio of peanuts to walnuts to pine nuts is 5:4:3. Which of the following could NOT be the total number of nuts in the basket?

    (A) 48
    (B) 64
    (C) 84
    (D) 144

23. For what values of $x$ does $\dfrac{x}{x+2} = \dfrac{4}{x(x+2)}$?

    (A) $x = -2$ only
    (B) $x = 0$ only
    (C) $x = 2$ only
    (D) $x = -2$ and $x = 0$ and $x = 2$

24. Which expression is equivalent to $\sqrt{50}$?

    (A) $5\sqrt{2}$
    (B) $2\sqrt{5}$
    (C) $5\sqrt{10}$
    (D) $10\sqrt{5}$

25. Which of the following expressions represents a negative number?

    (A) $4 - \pi$
    (B) $4 + \pi$
    (C) $\pi - 3$
    (D) $3 - \pi$

# MA

26. The grid below shows 3 vertices of a rectangle.

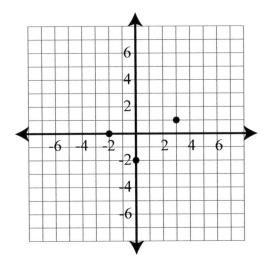

What are the coordinates of the fourth vertex of the rectangle?

(A) $(5, -1)$
(B) $(1, 3)$
(C) $(2, 2)$
(D) $(-5, -3)$

27. Which graph represents the solution set of the disjunction $r < -r$ or $r - 4 > -r$?

(A) 
-10 -8 -6 -4 -2 0 2 4 6 8 10

(B) 
-10 -8 -6 -4 -2 0 2 4 6 8 10

(C) 
-10 -8 -6 -4 -2 0 2 4 6 8 10

(D) 
-10 -8 -6 -4 -2 0 2 4 6 8 10

28. A trapezoid is a four-sided figure with two parallel bases. The area of a trapezoid is given by $A = \frac{1}{2}(b_1 + b_2)h$, where $b_1$ and $b_2$ are the lengths of the two bases and $h$ is the height. Trapezoid X has an area of 22 square units and a height of 4 units. One of Trapezoid X's bases is 5 units long. How long is the other base?

(A) 5 units
(B) 6 units
(C) 7 units
(D) 11 units

29. A deck contains cards labeled with one, two, three or four dots. A random card from this deck is drawn. The probability of each outcome is given below.

| Number of dots on card drawn | Probability |
| --- | --- |
| 1 | .3 |
| 2 | .1 |
| 3 | .2 |
| 4 | .4 |

What is the expected number of dots on the card?

(A) 2.4
(B) 2.5
(C) 2.6
(D) 2.7

30. The figure shows a rectangle, a portion of which is shaded.

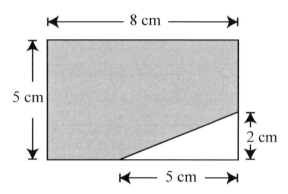

What is the area of the shaded portion?

(A) 30.0 cm²

(B) 32.0 cm²

(C) 35.0 cm²

(D) 37.5 cm²

31. The following stem-and-leaf plot represents the mass in grams of candies in a bowl.

| Stem | Leaf | | |
|------|------|---|---|
| 0 | 1 | 2 | 4 |
| 1 | 0 | 1 | |
| 2 | 5 | | |
| 3 | 1 | | |

What is the mean mass in grams of candies in the bowl?

(A) 13

(B) 12

(C) 11

(D) 10

32. If $x \neq 0$ and $y \neq 0$, which expression is equivalent to the expression $-\dfrac{2x^2 y}{xy^2}$?

(A) $-2$

(B) $-2xy$

(C) $2x^{-1}y$

(D) $-2xy^{-1}$

33. Triangle ABC is shown.

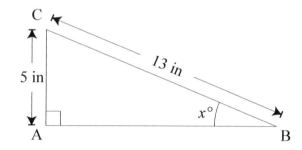

What is the value of $\tan x°$?

(A) $\dfrac{5}{13}$

(B) $\dfrac{12}{13}$

(C) $\dfrac{5}{12}$

(D) $\dfrac{12}{5}$

34. Which value is NOT equal to $.1\bar{6}$?

(A) $16\dfrac{2}{3}\%$

(B) $.1 + .06 + .006$

(C) $\dfrac{1}{6}$

(D) $.1 + .0\bar{6}$

35. Madelyn has the following data set:

$3, 4, 7, 3, 3, 5, 6, 6, 7, x, y$

She knows the value of $x$ and $y$ and uses all 11 values in the set to make the frequency bar chart below:

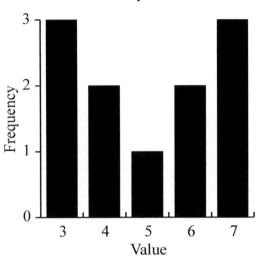

Madelyn's Data

What is the mean of $x$ and $y$?

(A) 4.0
(B) 5.0
(C) 5.5
(D) 7.0

36. Simon spends 30% more time studying than Norah does. If Simon spends 15 more minutes studying than Norah, how many minutes does Simon spend studying?

(A) 75
(B) 65
(C) 60
(D) 50

37. The figure shows a regular pentagon with one side extended.

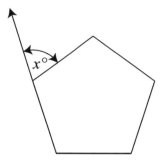

What is the value of $x$?

(A) 68
(B) 70
(C) 72
(D) 74

38. At a school event, there are twice as many 8th graders as 7th graders and twice as many 7th graders as 6th graders. If all students at the event are in 6th, 7th, or 8th grade, what fraction of the students are 8th graders?

(A) $\frac{1}{2}$

(B) $\frac{4}{7}$

(C) $\frac{5}{8}$

(D) $\frac{3}{4}$

39. Exactly one point on a circle lies on the *x*-axis in the standard *xy* plane. Which of the following could NOT be the center of the circle?

   (A) $(0, -1)$
   (B) $(-1, 0)$
   (C) $(1, -1)$
   (D) $(-1, 1)$

40. A machine produces 4 different types of bolts. The bolts weigh 1 gram, 10 grams, 100 grams and 1000 grams, respectively. Each day, the machine produces fewer than ten of each type of bolt. If the total weight of bolts produced by the machine yesterday was 9352 grams, how many bolts did the machine produce yesterday?

   (A) 14
   (B) 17
   (C) 19
   (D) The number of bolts cannot be determined from the information given

41. A bag contains 22 coins: 7 dimes, 9 nickels and 6 quarters. Silas randomly draws one coin from the bag and keeps it. Gabriela then prepares to select a random coin from the bag. If the probability that Gabriela selects a nickel is $\frac{8}{21}$, what type of coin did Silas draw from the bag?

   (A) a nickel
   (B) a dime
   (C) a quarter
   (D) there isn't enough information to determine the type of coin that Silas selected.

42. The chart below shows the accumulation of rainfall during a rainstorm.

| Time (hours since the start of the storm) | Rainfall (centimeters) |
|---|---|
| 0 | 0 |
| 1 | .7 |
| 2 | 1.4 |
| 3 | 2.1 |

Which of the following graphs best represents the given data?

(A)
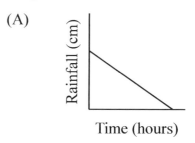

(B)
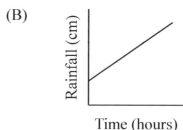

(C)
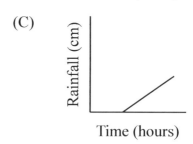

(D)
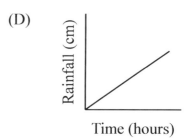

**STOP. If there is time, you may check your work in this section only.**

# Essay Directions

There is an essay topic printed on the next page of this test. Do not turn the page until you are told to begin. Once you are told to begin, you will have 30 minutes to write an essay on the topic provided. You may not write on another topic.

Your writing should be as clear as possible. The quality of your writing is more important than the length of your essay, but your essay should be long enough to develop your ideas and to demonstrate your writing ability.

You may plan your response in the notes section provided on the next page. Any writing you do in the notes section will NOT be counted as part of your essay. Your final draft must be written on the lined portion of your answer sheet. Only what is written on your answer sheet will be considered part of your essay. Remember that you will have only 30 minutes to plan and write your essay, so you should leave enough time to copy your final draft to the answer sheet.

Please use a blue or black pen to write your essay. Do not write outside of the box provided on the answer sheet. You may write in cursive or in print.

Please copy the following topic onto the first few lines of your answer sheet.

## Essay Topic

**Give an example of a good choice you have made. Why was it a good choice?**

- Do not write on any other topic.
- Write your final draft on the answer sheet, NOT in the space below.
- Write in blue or black pen.

### Notes

_____

_____

_____

_____

_____

_____

_____

_____

_____

_____

_____

_____

_____

_____

_____

_____

_____

# ISEE
Independent School Entrance Exam

# Practice Test 5

# Answer Sheet

## Verbal Reasoning

| | | | | | |
|---|---|---|---|---|---|
| 1 Ⓐ Ⓑ Ⓒ Ⓓ | 13 Ⓐ Ⓑ Ⓒ Ⓓ | 25 Ⓐ Ⓑ Ⓒ Ⓓ |
| 2 Ⓐ Ⓑ Ⓒ Ⓓ | 14 Ⓐ Ⓑ Ⓒ Ⓓ | 26 Ⓐ Ⓑ Ⓒ Ⓓ |
| 3 Ⓐ Ⓑ Ⓒ Ⓓ | 15 Ⓐ Ⓑ Ⓒ Ⓓ | 27 Ⓐ Ⓑ Ⓒ Ⓓ |
| 4 Ⓐ Ⓑ Ⓒ Ⓓ | 16 Ⓐ Ⓑ Ⓒ Ⓓ | 28 Ⓐ Ⓑ Ⓒ Ⓓ |
| 5 Ⓐ Ⓑ Ⓒ Ⓓ | 17 Ⓐ Ⓑ Ⓒ Ⓓ | 29 Ⓐ Ⓑ Ⓒ Ⓓ |
| 6 Ⓐ Ⓑ Ⓒ Ⓓ | 18 Ⓐ Ⓑ Ⓒ Ⓓ | 30 Ⓐ Ⓑ Ⓒ Ⓓ |
| 7 Ⓐ Ⓑ Ⓒ Ⓓ | 19 Ⓐ Ⓑ Ⓒ Ⓓ | 31 Ⓐ Ⓑ Ⓒ Ⓓ |
| 8 Ⓐ Ⓑ Ⓒ Ⓓ | 20 Ⓐ Ⓑ Ⓒ Ⓓ | 32 Ⓐ Ⓑ Ⓒ Ⓓ |
| 9 Ⓐ Ⓑ Ⓒ Ⓓ | 21 Ⓐ Ⓑ Ⓒ Ⓓ | 33 Ⓐ Ⓑ Ⓒ Ⓓ |
| 10 Ⓐ Ⓑ Ⓒ Ⓓ | 22 Ⓐ Ⓑ Ⓒ Ⓓ | 34 Ⓐ Ⓑ Ⓒ Ⓓ |
| 11 Ⓐ Ⓑ Ⓒ Ⓓ | 23 Ⓐ Ⓑ Ⓒ Ⓓ | 35 Ⓐ Ⓑ Ⓒ Ⓓ |
| 12 Ⓐ Ⓑ Ⓒ Ⓓ | 24 Ⓐ Ⓑ Ⓒ Ⓓ | |

## Quantitative Reasoning

| | | | | | |
|---|---|---|---|---|---|
| 1 Ⓐ Ⓑ Ⓒ Ⓓ | 12 Ⓐ Ⓑ Ⓒ Ⓓ | 23 Ⓐ Ⓑ Ⓒ Ⓓ |
| 2 Ⓐ Ⓑ Ⓒ Ⓓ | 13 Ⓐ Ⓑ Ⓒ Ⓓ | 24 Ⓐ Ⓑ Ⓒ Ⓓ |
| 3 Ⓐ Ⓑ Ⓒ Ⓓ | 14 Ⓐ Ⓑ Ⓒ Ⓓ | 25 Ⓐ Ⓑ Ⓒ Ⓓ |
| 4 Ⓐ Ⓑ Ⓒ Ⓓ | 15 Ⓐ Ⓑ Ⓒ Ⓓ | 26 Ⓐ Ⓑ Ⓒ Ⓓ |
| 5 Ⓐ Ⓑ Ⓒ Ⓓ | 16 Ⓐ Ⓑ Ⓒ Ⓓ | 27 Ⓐ Ⓑ Ⓒ Ⓓ |
| 6 Ⓐ Ⓑ Ⓒ Ⓓ | 17 Ⓐ Ⓑ Ⓒ Ⓓ | 28 Ⓐ Ⓑ Ⓒ Ⓓ |
| 7 Ⓐ Ⓑ Ⓒ Ⓓ | 18 Ⓐ Ⓑ Ⓒ Ⓓ | 29 Ⓐ Ⓑ Ⓒ Ⓓ |
| 8 Ⓐ Ⓑ Ⓒ Ⓓ | 19 Ⓐ Ⓑ Ⓒ Ⓓ | 30 Ⓐ Ⓑ Ⓒ Ⓓ |
| 9 Ⓐ Ⓑ Ⓒ Ⓓ | 20 Ⓐ Ⓑ Ⓒ Ⓓ | 31 Ⓐ Ⓑ Ⓒ Ⓓ |
| 10 Ⓐ Ⓑ Ⓒ Ⓓ | 21 Ⓐ Ⓑ Ⓒ Ⓓ | 32 Ⓐ Ⓑ Ⓒ Ⓓ |
| 11 Ⓐ Ⓑ Ⓒ Ⓓ | 22 Ⓐ Ⓑ Ⓒ Ⓓ | |

## Reading Comprehension

| | | | | | |
|---|---|---|---|---|---|
| 1 Ⓐ Ⓑ Ⓒ Ⓓ | 11 Ⓐ Ⓑ Ⓒ Ⓓ | 21 Ⓐ Ⓑ Ⓒ Ⓓ |
| 2 Ⓐ Ⓑ Ⓒ Ⓓ | 12 Ⓐ Ⓑ Ⓒ Ⓓ | 22 Ⓐ Ⓑ Ⓒ Ⓓ |
| 3 Ⓐ Ⓑ Ⓒ Ⓓ | 13 Ⓐ Ⓑ Ⓒ Ⓓ | 23 Ⓐ Ⓑ Ⓒ Ⓓ |
| 4 Ⓐ Ⓑ Ⓒ Ⓓ | 14 Ⓐ Ⓑ Ⓒ Ⓓ | 24 Ⓐ Ⓑ Ⓒ Ⓓ |
| 5 Ⓐ Ⓑ Ⓒ Ⓓ | 15 Ⓐ Ⓑ Ⓒ Ⓓ | 25 Ⓐ Ⓑ Ⓒ Ⓓ |
| 6 Ⓐ Ⓑ Ⓒ Ⓓ | 16 Ⓐ Ⓑ Ⓒ Ⓓ | 26 Ⓐ Ⓑ Ⓒ Ⓓ |
| 7 Ⓐ Ⓑ Ⓒ Ⓓ | 17 Ⓐ Ⓑ Ⓒ Ⓓ | 27 Ⓐ Ⓑ Ⓒ Ⓓ |
| 8 Ⓐ Ⓑ Ⓒ Ⓓ | 18 Ⓐ Ⓑ Ⓒ Ⓓ | 28 Ⓐ Ⓑ Ⓒ Ⓓ |
| 9 Ⓐ Ⓑ Ⓒ Ⓓ | 19 Ⓐ Ⓑ Ⓒ Ⓓ | 29 Ⓐ Ⓑ Ⓒ Ⓓ |
| 10 Ⓐ Ⓑ Ⓒ Ⓓ | 20 Ⓐ Ⓑ Ⓒ Ⓓ | 30 Ⓐ Ⓑ Ⓒ Ⓓ |

## Mathematics Achievement

| | | | | | |
|---|---|---|---|---|---|
| 1 Ⓐ Ⓑ Ⓒ Ⓓ | 15 Ⓐ Ⓑ Ⓒ Ⓓ | 29 Ⓐ Ⓑ Ⓒ Ⓓ |
| 2 Ⓐ Ⓑ Ⓒ Ⓓ | 16 Ⓐ Ⓑ Ⓒ Ⓓ | 30 Ⓐ Ⓑ Ⓒ Ⓓ |
| 3 Ⓐ Ⓑ Ⓒ Ⓓ | 17 Ⓐ Ⓑ Ⓒ Ⓓ | 31 Ⓐ Ⓑ Ⓒ Ⓓ |
| 4 Ⓐ Ⓑ Ⓒ Ⓓ | 18 Ⓐ Ⓑ Ⓒ Ⓓ | 32 Ⓐ Ⓑ Ⓒ Ⓓ |
| 5 Ⓐ Ⓑ Ⓒ Ⓓ | 19 Ⓐ Ⓑ Ⓒ Ⓓ | 33 Ⓐ Ⓑ Ⓒ Ⓓ |
| 6 Ⓐ Ⓑ Ⓒ Ⓓ | 20 Ⓐ Ⓑ Ⓒ Ⓓ | 34 Ⓐ Ⓑ Ⓒ Ⓓ |
| 7 Ⓐ Ⓑ Ⓒ Ⓓ | 21 Ⓐ Ⓑ Ⓒ Ⓓ | 35 Ⓐ Ⓑ Ⓒ Ⓓ |
| 8 Ⓐ Ⓑ Ⓒ Ⓓ | 22 Ⓐ Ⓑ Ⓒ Ⓓ | 36 Ⓐ Ⓑ Ⓒ Ⓓ |
| 9 Ⓐ Ⓑ Ⓒ Ⓓ | 23 Ⓐ Ⓑ Ⓒ Ⓓ | 37 Ⓐ Ⓑ Ⓒ Ⓓ |
| 10 Ⓐ Ⓑ Ⓒ Ⓓ | 24 Ⓐ Ⓑ Ⓒ Ⓓ | 38 Ⓐ Ⓑ Ⓒ Ⓓ |
| 11 Ⓐ Ⓑ Ⓒ Ⓓ | 25 Ⓐ Ⓑ Ⓒ Ⓓ | 39 Ⓐ Ⓑ Ⓒ Ⓓ |
| 12 Ⓐ Ⓑ Ⓒ Ⓓ | 26 Ⓐ Ⓑ Ⓒ Ⓓ | 40 Ⓐ Ⓑ Ⓒ Ⓓ |
| 13 Ⓐ Ⓑ Ⓒ Ⓓ | 27 Ⓐ Ⓑ Ⓒ Ⓓ | 41 Ⓐ Ⓑ Ⓒ Ⓓ |
| 14 Ⓐ Ⓑ Ⓒ Ⓓ | 28 Ⓐ Ⓑ Ⓒ Ⓓ | 42 Ⓐ Ⓑ Ⓒ Ⓓ |

# Answer Sheet - Essay

Write your response in blue or black pen.

STUDENT NAME  _____

Write your essay topic here.

_____
_____
_____

Write your response here.

_____
_____
_____
_____
_____
_____
_____
_____
_____
_____
_____
_____
_____
_____
_____
_____
_____
_____
_____
_____
_____
_____
_____
_____

(Answer Sheet - Essay continued)

# ISEE
Independent School Entrance Exam

# Upper Level
# Verbal Reasoning

# Practice Test 5

*This page intentionally left blank.*

# VR

## Section 1
## Verbal Reasoning

| 35 Questions | Time: 17.5 minutes |

This section is divided into two parts that contain two different types of questions. As soon as you have completed Part One, answer the questions in Part Two. You may write in your test booklet. For each answer you select, fill in the corresponding circle on your answer document.

## Part One — Synonyms

Each question in Part One consists of a word in capital letters followed by four answer choices. Select the one word that is most nearly the same in meaning as the word in capital letters.

---

SAMPLE QUESTION:                                             SAMPLE ANSWER:

EXTEND:                                                      Ⓐ ● Ⓒ Ⓓ

   (A) avoid

   (B) lengthen

   (C) criticize

   (D) discover

---

## Part Two — Sentence Completion

Each question in Part Two is made up of a sentence with one or two blanks. One blank indicates that one word is missing. Two blanks indicate that two words are missing. Each sentence is followed by four answer choices. Select the one word or pair of words that best completes the meaning of the sentence as a whole.

---

SAMPLE QUESTIONS:                                           SAMPLE ANSWERS:

Unlike her older brother, who always acted --------,        ● Ⓑ Ⓒ Ⓓ
Cheryl preferred to take her time.

   (A) quickly

   (B) carefully

   (C) stupidly

   (D) wisely


Whitewater rafting is both ------- and dangerous: rapids    Ⓐ Ⓑ Ⓒ ●
may provide thrills, but they also threaten a rafter's ------.

   (A) ancient...pride

   (B) understandable...judgment

   (C) informative...freedom

   (D) exciting...safety

---

STOP. Do not go on
until told to do so.   **STOP**

# Part One — Synonyms

**Directions:** Select the word that is most nearly the same in meaning as the word in capital letters.

1. VULGAR:

(A) hurtful
(B) rude
(C) careless
(D) proper

2. NOURISH:

(A) feed
(B) multiply
(C) filter
(D) brace

3. MALICIOUS:

(A) distasteful
(B) intentional
(C) mean
(D) admirable

4. FEUD:

(A) incentive
(B) lubricant
(C) mist
(D) argument

5. DEVOUR:

(A) clutch
(B) consume
(C) broaden
(D) share

6. PREJUDICE:

(A) hatred
(B) corruption
(C) charity
(D) bias

7. FRAGMENT:

(A) sliver
(B) weapon
(C) failure
(D) projectile

8. DOCTRINE:

(A) assistance
(B) garbage
(C) ideology
(D) maneuver

9. ENCOMPASS:

(A) guide
(B) swerve
(C) disguise
(D) contain

10. CONVEY:

(A) manufacture
(B) transport
(C) supply
(D) invest

11. NIMBLE:

(A) agile
(B) miniature
(C) weak
(D) adequate

12. EXTRICATE:

(A) disengage
(B) entangle
(C) warp
(D) explain

13. COVET:

(A) protect
(B) neutralize
(C) desire
(D) hide

14. PENITENT:

(A) confined
(B) apologetic
(C) elderly
(D) immune

15. VIABLE:

(A) competitive
(B) receptive
(C) responsible
(D) workable

16. SAVORY:

(A) liberating
(B) appetizing
(C) descriptive
(D) eternal

17. ARTISAN:

(A) scribe
(B) aristocrat
(C) inventor
(D) craftsman

## Part Two — Sentence Completion

**Directions:** Select the word or word pair that best completes the sentence.

18. In an attempt to decode the mysteries of ancient Egyptian writings, scholars have ------- computers running sophisticated algorithms for processing language.

    (A) uncovered
    (B) referenced
    (C) reduced
    (D) employed

19. During the interview process, a few minor mistakes do not usually disqualify a job candidate; Sheila, however, made so many ------- that her interviewers simply could not take her seriously.

    (A) provocations
    (B) blunders
    (C) prescriptions
    (D) arguments

20. Some comedians rely on ------- for easy laughs, but Sufjan avoids such oversimplified, formulaic portraits in creating his humor.

    (A) stereotypes
    (B) vulgarities
    (C) retorts
    (D) pranks

21. Ellington, alone in the woods and face to face with an aggressive wolverine, found he could keep the animal at bay by ------- his tent pole as a weapon.

    (A) brandishing
    (B) mangling
    (C) retaining
    (D) conquering

22. In *The Great Gatsby*, F. Scott Fitzgerald paints the ------- of the 1920s in fine strokes, capturing the lavish parties and loose morals of the wealthy Long Island elite with eloquent precision.

    (A) stubbornness
    (B) superiority
    (C) mediocrity
    (D) decadence

23. Though designed to alleviate cold symptoms, the drug actually ------- patients' nasal congestion and throat irritation.

    (A) lessened
    (B) counteracted
    (C) softened
    (D) exacerbated

24. Tired of hearing sugarcoated reports from her senior staff, chief executive Marissa Mayer appealed directly to her engineers for a ------- assessment of the project's progress.

    (A) superficial
    (B) candid
    (C) derisive
    (D) favorable

25. Develin felt ------- about seeing his mother, for it seemed to him that every conversation between the two ended in a bitter argument.

    (A) thrilled
    (B) jubilant
    (C) defensive
    (D) apprehensive

26. Dark, thick clouds in the distance are an ------- sign for hikers on the exposed west face of Mount McKinley.

    (A) inspiring
    (B) obscure
    (C) ominous
    (D) insignificant

27. After advertising on television failed to attract attention, advocates of reform tried a different -------: handing out leaflets in front of local grocery stores.

    (A) resolution
    (B) vocation
    (C) tactic
    (D) engagement

28. Lyndon Johnson was a ------- supporter of equal rights, never ------- in his commitment to justice for all Americans, regardless of color.

    (A) fickle...hesitating
    (B) reliable...proceeding
    (C) steady...wavering
    (D) hesitant...pausing

29. Conservative communities are less likely to tolerate ------- attitudes than ------- communities are.

    (A) reactionary...liberal
    (B) old-fashioned...peaceful
    (C) radical...progressive
    (D) conventional...moderate

30. Participants in pickup ultimate frisbee have a range of ability levels, from fresh-faced ------- to highly experienced -------.

    (A) novices...veterans
    (B) newcomers...pupils
    (C) experts...beginners
    (D) enthusiasts...spectators

31. One can view social dance as a -------, spanning the gap between generations and bringing together otherwise ------- individuals.

    (A) bridge...lonely
    (B) bond...irritable
    (C) connection...outgoing
    (D) panacea...coarse

32. On the question of whether musical talent is learned or -------, experts -------; some argue that it develops only with practice, while others contend that it is embedded in our genes.

   (A) natural...concur
   (B) innate...differ
   (C) acquired...sympathize
   (D) compliant...diverge

33. Though ------- during his lifetime, Gregor Mendel received ------- recognition for his insight into patterns of inheritance.

   (A) unappreciated...contemporary
   (B) celebrated...prominent
   (C) reclusive...improper
   (D) unknown...posthumous

34. The ceremony was a humorless affair, filled with ------- speeches and lacking any -------.

   (A) witty...pretension
   (B) stern...mirth
   (C) lengthy...gravity
   (D) absurd...urgency

35. Martin ------- professed his love for Eliza, but she was put off by his ------- declarations.

   (A) eagerly...fervent
   (B) passionately...tepid
   (C) helplessly...irresistible
   (D) ardently...morose

STOP. Do not go on until told to do so.

# ISEE
Independent School Entrance Exam

# Upper Level
# Quantitative Reasoning

# Practice Test 5

# Section 2
# Quantitative Reasoning

| 32 Questions | Time: 30 minutes |

This section has two parts that contain two different kinds of questions. Do not pause after Part One. Continue working through Part Two. You may write in your test booklet.

Letters such as $x$ and $y$ stand for real numbers. All figures are drawn to scale unless otherwise stated.

**Part One — Word Problems**

Each question in Part One consists of a word problem followed by four answer choices. Select the best answer from the four choices given and fill in the corresponding circle on your answer document.

---

EXAMPLE 1:　　　　　　　　　　　　　　　　SAMPLE ANSWER

Ⓐ Ⓑ Ⓒ ●

Which of the following fractions is greater than $\frac{3}{4}$?

(A) $\frac{1}{5}$

(B) $\frac{1}{4}$

(C) $\frac{2}{5}$

(D) $\frac{4}{5}$

The correct answer is $\frac{4}{5}$, so circle D is darkened.

---

*Go on to the next page.* ➡

# QR

**2**

## Part Two — Quantitative Comparisons

In Part Two, use the given information to compare the quantities given in Column A and Column B. Choose one of these four answer choices:

        (A)  The quantity in Column A is greater.
        (B)  The quantity in Column B is greater.
        (C)  The two quantities are equal.
        (D)  The relationship cannot be determined from the information given.

---

EXAMPLE 2:

| Column A | Column B |
|---|---|
| The greatest integer that is less than 4.1 | The smallest integer that is greater than 3.9 |

SAMPLE ANSWER

Ⓐ Ⓑ ● Ⓓ

The quantity in Column A (4) is the same as the quantity in Column B (4), so circle C is darkened.

---

EXAMPLE 3:

$$x^2 > 4$$

| Column A | Column B |
|---|---|
| $x$ | 2 |

SAMPLE ANSWER

Ⓐ Ⓑ Ⓒ ●

One possible value for $x$ is 3 because $3^2 = 9$ and $9 > 4$. Another possible value for $x$ is $-3$ because $(-3)^2 = 9$ also. Because the quantity in Column A (3 or $-3$, for instance) may be greater than or less than the quantity in Column B (2), the relationship cannot be determined and circle D is darkened.

STOP. Do not go on until told to do so. **STOP**

## Part One — Word Problems

**Directions:** Choose the best answer from the four choices given.

1. If $y + 3z = 2$, then which expression is equal to $z$?

   (A) $\dfrac{y-2}{3}$

   (B) $\dfrac{2-y}{3}$

   (C) $\dfrac{2}{3} - y$

   (D) $\dfrac{2}{y} - 3$

2. In a test, a car is driven at $s$ miles per hour for $h$ hours, traveling a distance of $d$ miles in the process. In a second test, the car is driven at $.6s$ miles per hour for $1.1h$ hours. During this second test, approximately what percent of the original distance $d$ does the car travel?

   (A) 50%
   (B) 60%
   (C) 66%
   (D) 170%

3. What is the value of the following expression?

   $$12 \times 351 - 349 \times 12$$

   (A) 24
   (B) 12
   (C) 3
   (D) 2

4. Juan's teacher asks him to calculate the mean, median, mode, and range of the following list of 10 numbers:

   $$51, 54, 54, 57, 57, 57, 57, 57, 61, 65$$

   Juan's teacher then adds a new number greater than 65 to the list. If Juan recalculates the mean, median and mode for this new list of 11 numbers, which of the following measurements has changed?

   (A) The range and the median
   (B) The mode and the mean
   (C) The range and the mean
   (D) The median and the mean

5. If the sum of all odd integers from 1 to 99 (inclusive) is $a$ and the sum of all odd integers from 5 to 97 (inclusive) is $b$, what is the value of $a - b$?

   (A) 4
   (B) 92
   (C) 94
   (D) 103

6. A survey asked 12 children how many television shows they watched. The results are shown below:

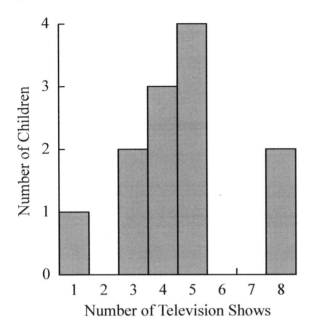

Which of the following statements is true?

(A) The mode of the data is 4.0
(B) The median of the data is 4.5
(C) The mode of the data is 2.0
(D) The median of the data is 4.0

7. The product of two positive integers is 225. What is the smallest possible sum of the integers?

(A) 30
(B) 34
(C) 50
(D) 78

8. Chris, Jen and Marcus are all running for the same seat on the student council. One of the three will win. If the probability that Chris wins is less than 50%, and the probability that Jen wins is less than 50%, which of the following events is most likely?

(A) Jen or Marcus wins
(B) Jen or Chris wins
(C) Chris or Marcus wins
(D) There isn't enough information given to determine the answer.

9. If $y = -3x^2 + 2$ and $-2 \leq x \leq 4$, what is the maximum possible value of $y$?

(A) $-46$
(B) $-10$
(C) $-1$
(D) $2$

10. Sarah and Allen walk toward each other along a straight path. Each walks at a constant rate. The distance between the two as a function of time is shown below.

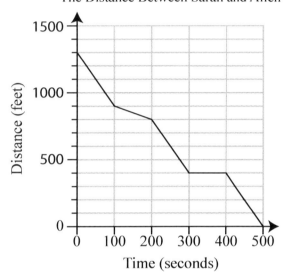

The Distance Between Sarah and Allen

At time $x$, both Sarah and Allen stop to rest. At time $y$, Sarah stops but Allen continues walking. How far apart are they at time $y$?

(A) 1300 feet
(B) 900 feet
(C) 800 feet
(D) 400 feet

11. If $n$ is an even integer, which of the following represents the greatest even integer that is less than $n$?

(A) $n + 2$
(B) $n + 1$
(C) $n - 2$
(D) $n - 1$

12. Both Courtney and Bekah run loops around a circular track. Courtney finishes each loop in 8 minutes and Bekah finishes each loop in 6 minutes. They leave the start line together and both stop running when they arrive at the start line together. How many loops does Courtney run?

(A) 8
(B) 6
(C) 4
(D) 3

13. Andre uses a 5 inch by 7 inch piece of paper to create a scale drawing of his rectangular garden. If the edges of the paper represent the boundaries of the garden, which of the following could NOT be the actual dimensions of the garden?

(A) 3 meters by 5 meters
(B) 2.5 feet by 3.5 feet
(C) 10 meters by 14 meters
(D) 50 feet by 70 feet

14. If the following equation is true for all values of $x$, what is the value of $a$?

$$\frac{10 + 7x}{14} = a + \frac{x}{2}$$

(A) $\dfrac{5}{7}$
(B) $\dfrac{7}{10}$
(C) $\dfrac{10}{7}$
(D) 2

15. Triangle PQR is similar to triangle STV.

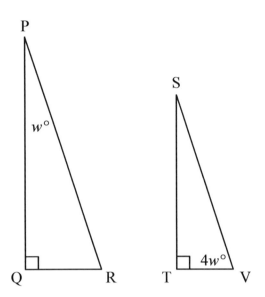

What is the measure of angle S?

(A)  18°

(B)  22.5°

(C)  4w°

(D)  (90–w)°

16. Ryan asked 30 of his friends to name their favorite desserts. He then made a circle graph representing the results of his survey.

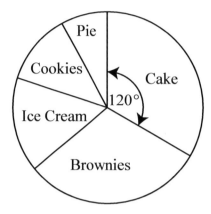

How many of Ryan's friends chose cake as their favorite dessert?

(A)  8

(B)  9

(C)  10

(D)  12

17. For 3 consecutive days last week, Anya recorded the temperature at noon. She found that the temperature on the first day was 70 degrees Fahrenheit, and it increased by two degrees each day after that. Which of the following is a plot of frequency versus temperature for the 3 days that Anya recorded?

(A)
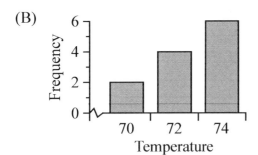

(B)
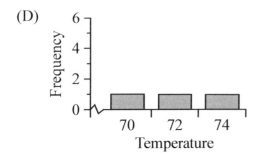

(C)

(D)

18. The shape shown below is a net of a solid.

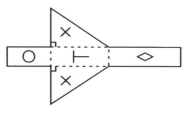

The shape could be a net for which of the following solids?

(A)
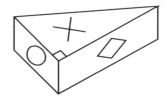

(B)
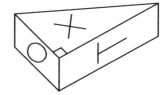

(C)
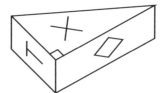

(D)
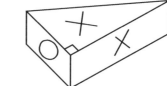

# QR

②

**Directions:** Using the information given in each question, compare the quantity in Column A to the quantity in Column B. All questions in Part Two have these answer choices:

(A)    The quantity in Column A is greater.
(B)    The quantity in Column B is greater.
(C)    The two quantities are equal.
(D)    The relationship cannot be determined from the information given.

---

| Column A | Column B |
|---|---|
| 19.    $-(x-5+y)$ | $5-y-x$ |

A number cube labeled 1-6 is thrown twice in a row.

| Column A | Column B |
|---|---|
| 20.  If the sum of the two throws is 4, the probability that the first roll was a 1 | If the sum of the two throws is 3, the probability that the first roll was a 1 |

The number of registered voters in Dillon county increased by 70% from 2004 to 2008. By 2012, the number of registered voters was more than twice what it was in 2004.

| Column A | Column B |
|---|---|
| 21.  The percent increase in registered voters from 2008 to 2012 | 30% |

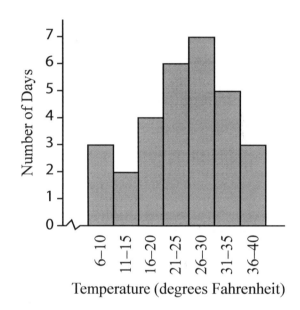

The histogram above shows the temperatures of the 30 days in January.

| Column A | Column B |
|---|---|
| 22.  The median temperature | 25.5 degrees |

**Answer choices for all questions on this page:**

(A) The quantity in Column A is greater.
(B) The quantity in Column B is greater.
(C) The two quantities are equal.
(D) The relationship cannot be determined from the information given.

| | Column A | Column B |
|---|---|---|
| 23. | $(8+3)^2 - (3-1)^2$ | $73 - 8$ |

Line $n$ passes through the point $(2, 1)$ and the origin. Line $m$ passes through the point $(-1, -2)$ and the origin.

| | Column A | Column B |
|---|---|---|
| 24. | The slope of line $n$ | The slope of line $m$ |

The product of three consecutive even integers is less than zero.

| | Column A | Column B |
|---|---|---|
| 25. | The product of the integers | The sum of the integers |

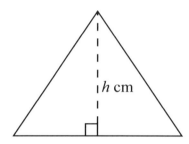

The figure shows an isosceles triangle with height $h$ centimeters.

| | Column A | Column B |
|---|---|---|
| 26. | The perimeter of the triangle | $2h$ cm |

$y$ is an integer between 0 and 9, inclusive.

| | Column A | Column B |
|---|---|---|
| 27. | $1 + .01y$ | $1.1 - .01(10 - y)$ |

**Answer choices for all questions on this page:**

(A) The quantity in Column A is greater.
(B) The quantity in Column B is greater.
(C) The two quantities are equal.
(D) The relationship cannot be determined from the information given.

In a bag of coins, there are equal numbers of dimes and quarters, and there are more nickels than quarters. (Note: 1 dime=$.10, 1 quarter=$.25 and 1 nickel=$.05)

| | Column A | Column B |
|---|---|---|
| 28. | The total value of the dimes and nickels together | The total value of the quarters |

A vertical tower stands on a flat plain, and an identical vertical tower stands on a nearby hill.

| | Column A | Column B |
|---|---|---|
| 29. | The distance between the bases of the towers | The distance between the tops of the towers |

The figure above is a semi-circle. The area of the semi-circle is $32\pi$ square inches.

| | Column A | Column B |
|---|---|---|
| 30. | The perimeter of the figure | 40 inches |

Holden is in a math class with some other students. The teacher calls on one randomly chosen student to answer a question, then calls on a different student to answer a second question.

| | Column A | Column B |
|---|---|---|
| 31. | The probability that the teacher calls on Holden first | If the teacher does not call on Holden first, the probability that the teach calls on Holden second |

| | Column A | Column B |
|---|---|---|
| 32. | $(a-b)^2$ | $a^2 - 2ab - b^2$ |

**STOP. If there is time, you may check your work in this section only.**

STOP

*This page intentionally left blank.*

# ISEE
## Independent School Entrance Exam

# Upper Level
# Reading Comprehension

# Practice Test 5

*This page intentionally left blank.*

# Section 3
# Reading Comprehension

**30 Questions**

**Time: 30 minutes**

This section contains five short reading passages. Each passage is followed by six questions based on its content. Answer the questions following each passage on the basis of what is stated or implied in that passage. You may write in your test booklet.

STOP. Do not go on
until told to do so.

**STOP**

Questions 1–6

1   The year was 1933, and the country
2   was mired in the darkest days of the Great
3   Depression. President Franklin Delano
4   Roosevelt had just taken office after a landslide
5   victory, promising a "New Deal" for the
6   American people. He seemed optimistic, but
7   for most hope was hard to find. Many were
8   on welfare, waiting in bread lines or at soup
9   kitchens. Others begged from door to door for
10  food or spare change to feed their families. One
11  out of every four workers was unemployed.
12      Seeking an active response to these
13  desperate times, the Roosevelt administration
14  created the Civilian Conservation Corps (CCC).
15  Roosevelt saw an opportunity to mobilize
16  hundreds of thousands of young men and put
17  them to work in the service of nature. This "Tree
18  Army," as it became known, would be stationed
19  in forests, parks, and rangelands throughout the
20  United States to complete projects that would
21  benefit both the land and CCC participants. In
22  a letter to Congress, Roosevelt wrote, "More
23  important, however, than the material gains, will
24  be the moral and spiritual value of such work."
25  It was a time when people needed not just a job
26  but a purpose.
27      The American people weren't the only ones
28  facing hard times. Across the country, poor
29  conservation, heavy use of natural resources,
30  and severe drought threatened the natural
31  landscape.  In Maine, one of the newer national
32  parks was struggling. Even though Acadia
33  National Park had recently celebrated its 17th
34  birthday, it was still rural, small, and

35  undeveloped. Unchecked growth of vegetation
36  prevented access to many areas, and the
37  facilities were inadequate for the park's large
38  number of visitors.
39      Superintendent George Dorr desperately
40  wanted to develop the area and saw a huge
41  opportunity in the CCC. He petitioned
42  Roosevelt for a camp to be stationed at
43  Acadia. His wish became reality when
44  one of the program's earliest camps was
45  established at Eagle Lake, the current site of
46  park headquarters. Soon a second camp was
47  established near Southwest Harbor, the Great
48  Pond Camp. Out of more than 4,000 camps that
49  would eventually be created nationally, only
50  100 would run the entire span of the program,
51  including the two in Acadia.  During the nine
52  years that CCC members labored at these two
53  camps, they completed hundreds of forestry
54  projects, such as fire fighting, fuel reduction,
55  and disease control. The "Tree Army" also
56  performed most of the work in constructing
57  the park's two campgrounds, Blackwoods
58  and Seawall. Its most enduring and endearing
59  successes, though, are the stunning and unusual
60  trails that lead hikers into the heart of Acadia.
61  Corps members cut granite blocks weighing
62  more than a ton and laid them on the trails
63  by hand. They cleared thousands of dead or
64  downed trees to open new paths into the forest.
65  The work was hard, but fulfilling, and through
66  their efforts, the CCC opened, protected, and
67  beautified Acadia National Park.

1.  The passage as a whole is best described as

    (A) a celebration of Franklin Delano Roosevelt's achievements
    (B) a warning about the dangers of unemployment
    (C) a history of the CCC and its relationship to Acadia
    (D) an assessment of a government agency

2.  The first paragraph provides

    (A) context for discussion of a topic
    (B) evidence for a claim
    (C) details of a public project
    (D) foreshadowing of an event

3.  As used in line 23, the word "material" most nearly means

    (A) fabric
    (B) valuable
    (C) relevant
    (D) tangible

4.  It can be inferred from the passage that the "entire span" of the CCC program was

    (A) less than 9 years
    (B) about 17 years
    (C) about 9 years
    (D) more than 17 years

5.  In context, which word best describes the "purpose" mentioned in line 26?

    (A) "enduring" (line 58)
    (B) "stunning" (line 59)
    (C) "hard" (line 65)
    (D) "fulfilling" (line 65)

6.  George Dorr wanted the CCC to be stationed at Acadia National Park because

    (A) the park needed more visitors
    (B) the facilities in the park were insufficient
    (C) local people needed employment
    (D) he wanted to make a profit

Questions 7–12

Just a few weeks ago, I celebrated my birthday. It was a small affair with family and friends, and we gathered to have a pleasant meal, some birthday cake and a birthday song. After dinner, my sister visited the kitchen to prepare the cake while the rest of the party lounged at the table, stuffed and satisfied. When she returned, though, she found the scene had changed. Conversation had dried up, Elan had left for the rest room, and those of us who remained sat quietly, lost in our smartphones.

I looked up to see a mixture of disappointment and exasperation in her eyes. Glancing around the room, I suddenly recognized the absurdity of the situation: here I sat with a number of those dearest to me, on one of those few occasions when we were able to be together for an evening, and yet we sat in silence. We had fallen victim to the appeal of those shiny, mesmerizing devices that we apparently cannot be without, even for an hour —devices that merely a decade before had not existed.

The advent of the smartphone has certainly made many aspects of our lives easier. We no longer fear being lost in an unfamiliar place. We can keep in touch with friends and family instantaneously and in a multitude of unexpected ways. Our fingers and our minds are constantly occupied, so that even the dullest moments—waiting in line at the grocery store, for instance—are easily filled with activity.

But the constant availability of diversions comes at the price of quality face-to-face interaction. There is an art to navigating the ebb and flow of a conversation. When a certain line of talk stalls, a skilled conversationalist seamlessly redirects to a new topic, creating a comfortable sense of togetherness with his companions. This apparent ease of transition is not an innate social talent but rather a practiced skill that we constantly hone in our daily interactions with others. The excuse of checking one's phone provides an all-too-easy retreat from the friction and awkwardness inherent in socializing. When we shrink from the little challenges of the casual exchange, our conversational skills (and with them, the richness of our social lives) slowly diminish.

7. As used in line 24, the word "advent" most nearly means

(A) season
(B) arrival
(C) intelligence
(D) occurrence

8. The passage does which of the following?

(A) describes an event, then draws a lesson from it
(B) states a principle, then mentions applications
(C) poses a question, then offers differing answers
(D) reflects on the past, then predicts the future

9. Overall, the author views smartphones as

(A) debilitating crutches
(B) helpful devices
(C) mixed blessings
(D) useless distractions

10. The author's sister feels "disappointment and exasperation" (line 13) in response to

(A) Elan's absence
(B) apparent laziness
(C) a messy table
(D) antisocial behavior

11. The passage states that making conversation is a

(A) natural ability
(B) learned skill
(C) waste of time
(D) forgotten art

12. The "little challenges of the casual exchange" (line 47) refers to

(A) difficulty with a business transaction
(B) discomfort in a social situation
(C) problems leaving a phone message
(D) anxiety about birthday presents

Questions 13–18

1   When I was old enough to earn money but
2   not old enough to have a proper job, I mowed
3   the Millers' lawn for ten dollars. The first mow
4   was a daunting task. The lawn, larger than it
5   had seemed at first, stretched around the house
6   and down a long slope to a flat portion by the
7   water's edge. Furthermore, no one had mown
8   it for what seemed like millennia, and the grass
9   rose to my knees.
10   I began with the level section surrounding
11   the house. There, my only obstacles were the
12   detritus of children's play: a rusty tricycle,
13   a miniature dump truck, some plastic balls.
14   Weeds had grown over and through the toys,
15   leaving them buried in the mountains of grass.
16   All of these objects were brightly colored,
17   though, and therefore easily spotted before a
18   collision.
19   I made a mistake in approaching the sloped
20   portion of the lawn: I mowed down the hill then
21   back up the hill. After two or three passes, my
22   legs burned, and my back ached. Only then
23   did it occur to me that by mowing back and
24   forth instead of up and down, I could avoid the
25   continual fight with gravity that so quickly wore
26   on my body.
27   When at last I made it to the bottom of the
28   hill, I was dismayed to find the ground on the
29   flat portion soft with water. The wheels of the
30   lawn mower sank into the earth, hampering
31   my progress and leaving muddy brown ruts in
32   the lawn in my wake. Not only that, but the
33   wet grass formed clumps on the interior of
34   the mower, repeatedly causing the mower to
35   stall. The machine had a pull-start engine that
36   required several forceful yanks to set in motion,
37   and soon my right shoulder was complaining
38   more loudly than my legs or my back.

13. The primary purpose of the passage is to

    (A) illustrate the hardships encountered while doing a job
    (B) explain why mowing the lawn was a bad idea
    (C) describe various ways in which the narrator made money as a child
    (D) point out that mowing lawns can cause injuries

14. In line 12, the word "detritus" most nearly means

    (A) remains
    (B) fragments
    (C) blockages
    (D) detriments

15. It can be inferred from the passage that the Millers' children

    (A) had played on the lawn recently
    (B) had played on the lawn some time ago
    (C) did not like their toys
    (D) were not supervised while playing

16. In the third paragraph (lines 19-26) the narrator

    (A) complains that the slope was very steep
    (B) observes that the ground on the slope was soft and wet
    (C) states that mowing back and forth caused a continual fight with gravity
    (D) describes first an inefficient way to mow, then a more efficient way

17. The mower's pull-start engine (lines 35-36) was particularly problematic for the narrator because

    (A) it was difficult to start the engine when the narrator first began mowing
    (B) the engine had to be restarted frequently in the wet conditions
    (C) the mower left muddy ruts in the wet ground
    (D) it was impossible to restart the engine once it had stalled

18. The use of the word "complaining" in line 37 is an example of

    (A) alliteration
    (B) exaggeration
    (C) personification
    (D) simile

Questions 19–24

1    Why is the Earth so restless? What causes
2  the ground to shake violently, volcanoes to
3  erupt with explosive force, and great mountain
4  ranges to rise to incredible heights? Scientists,
5  philosophers, and theologians have wrestled
6  with questions such as these for centuries.
7    Until the 1700s, most Europeans thought
8  that a single great flood played a major role
9  in shaping the Earth's surface. This way of
10  thinking was known as "catastrophism," and
11  geology was based on the belief that all earthly
12  changes were sudden and caused by a series of
13  catastrophes. However, by the mid-19<sup>th</sup> century,
14  catastrophism gave way to "uniformitarianism,"
15  a new way of thinking centered around the
16  "Uniformitarian Principle" proposed in 1785
17  by James Hutton, a Scottish geologist. This
18  principle is commonly stated as follows: The
19  present is the key to the past. Those holding this
20  viewpoint assume that the geologic forces and
21  processes—gradual as well as catastrophic—
22  acting on the Earth today are the same as those
23  that have acted in the geologic past.
24    Hutton's idea influenced both the theory
25  of continental drift and its successor, the
26  modern theory of plate tectonics. According
27  to both theories, the present day continents
28  are the fragmented pieces of preexisting larger
29  landmasses. The theory of continental drift
30  suggested that continents move around the

31  surface of the earth, but it did not offer an
32  explanation of the mechanism that causes the
33  movement.
34    The theory of plate tectonics, on the other
35  hand, proposes such a mechanism. Plate
36  tectonics states that the Earth's outermost layer
37  is fragmented into a dozen or more large and
38  small plates that move relative to one another
39  as they ride atop hotter, more mobile material.
40  The motion of the plates (and consequently
41  the continents) is primarily driven by the heat
42  energy present in the molten rock beneath the
43  plates. This energy may manifest itself in the
44  form of convection currents that we cannot
45  directly observe or more spectacular displays
46  such as earthquakes and volcanic eruptions.
47    Plate tectonics is a relatively new scientific
48  concept, introduced some 50 years ago, but it
49  has revolutionized our understanding of the
50  dynamic planet upon which we live. The theory
51  has unified the study of the Earth by drawing
52  together many branches of the earth sciences,
53  from paleontology (the study of fossils) to
54  seismology (the study of earthquakes). It
55  has provided explanations for questions that
56  scientists had speculated upon for centuries—
57  such as why earthquakes and volcanic eruptions
58  occur in very specific areas around the world,
59  and how and why great mountain ranges like the
60  Alps and Himalayas formed.

19. Those who follow the "Uniformitarian Principle" (line 16) believe that past geologic changes

    (A) happened only gradually
    (B) were mostly caused by catastrophes
    (C) took place in a narrow span of time
    (D) are like today's changes

20. The passage defines all of the following terms EXCEPT

    (A) paleontology
    (B) plate tectonics
    (C) catastrophism
    (D) theologians

21. The passage implies the theory of continental drift

    (A) has brought together many different sciences
    (B) incorrectly assumed that continents have fragmented over time
    (C) was replaced by the theory of plate tectonics
    (D) should be taken seriously

22. The second paragraph (lines 7-23) provides examples of

    (A) different viewpoints
    (B) discredited theories
    (C) rival scholars
    (D) complementary ideas

23. The main purpose of the passage is to

    (A) celebrate recent breakthroughs in geology
    (B) discuss alternatives to plate tectonics
    (C) introduce plate tectonics with historical context
    (D) show how the sciences have changed since the 1700s

24. The overall tone of the passage is best described as

    (A) instructive
    (B) uncertain
    (C) argumentative
    (D) humorous

Questions 25–30

1    "What do you do with a B.A. in English?"
2    So begins a song from a famous Broadway
3    musical. The question apparently bothers
4    more and more undergraduates in the real
5    world also. The humanities—philosophy,
6    literature, religion, and other studies of human
7    culture—have fallen out of fashion in higher
8    education. In their place, engineering, business,
9    mathematics and computer science have grown
10   in popularity. These are seen as the practical
11   disciplines, ones that promise a return on the
12   considerable financial investment that a college
13   education represents.
14   While the world no doubt needs computer
15   scientists and engineers, we should reflect
16   on the value that the study of the humanities
17   provides as well. The superficial argument for
18   the humanities is an economic one: the human
19   touch is necessary to run a successful business,
20   and therefore humanities students will satisfy
21   certain needs of the business world. A computer
22   programmer can create the software to run a
23   news website, but a writer must fill the site with
24   meaningful content. An engineer may develop a
25   revolutionary device, but only an understanding
26   of people and their interactions with technology
27   can make the device successful.
28   This economic argument, though appealing
29   to some parents who are concerned for their
30   children's future job prospects, misses the point
31   entirely. Surely if a student's primary goal is to
32   make money, the humanities are not the right

33   place to be. Another argument, then, for the
34   value of the humanities is a civic one: as
35   participants in a democracy, we must be
36   prepared to make informed judgments about
37   important issues of the day. For example, when
38   casting a vote for a politician who supports
39   armed intervention abroad, we must be able
40   to ask ourselves whether that intervention is
41   justified and worthwhile. When considering
42   a referendum on school reform, we must
43   understand the needs of our children and our
44   society. People with a background in the
45   humanities are better equipped to handle such
46   judgments.
47   Although there is some truth to this civic-
48   responsibility argument, it requires the unlikely
49   assumption that students will focus on the
50   greater good rather than their own interests
51   when choosing a major. So instead of the
52   economic argument or the civic-responsibility
53   argument, I suggest a simpler one: the
54   humanities are good for our souls. Reflection
55   on what it means to be human makes us better
56   people. The humanist grapples with fear and
57   courage, pride and humility, right and wrong,
58   joy and sorrow. In so doing, she becomes a
59   stronger friend and more caring neighbor. When
60   she passes on, she is remembered not for the
61   dollar value of the trust she leaves to her son,
62   but for the impact she has had on his character.
63   This, then, is the value of the humanities: they
64   instruct us in how best to live our lives.

25. In the third and fourth paragraphs (lines 14-46) the author

    (A) gives examples related to his topic
    (B) considers two arguments that he ultimately rejects
    (C) recalls his own parents' advice
    (D) contrasts two approaches to a problem

26. The author introduces his essay with all of the following EXCEPT

    (A) a motivating question
    (B) a direct quotation
    (C) an outside reference
    (D) a sensory description

27. Of the following possible titles, which one best captures the main topic of the passage?

    (A) "Why We Study the Humanities"
    (B) "Humanities Majors in Business"
    (C) "Responsible Citizenship and the Humanities"
    (D) "Practical Undergraduate Majors"

28. According to the passage, a person with a background in the humanities is most likely to

    (A) make plenty of money
    (B) cast well-informed votes
    (C) invent a new device
    (D) have children

29. Why is "the humanist" (line 56) a good friend and neighbor?

    (A) she understands people's emotions
    (B) she treats everyone with kindness
    (C) she is old and wise
    (D) she helps others improve their lives

30. According to the "superficial argument" (line 17), businesses need

    (A) computer programmers to create content
    (B) engineers to interact with technology
    (C) humanities students to write news stories
    (D) software to keep track of sales

STOP. If there is time, you may check your work on this section only.

STOP

*This page intentionally left blank.*

# ISEE
### Independent School Entrance Exam

# Upper Level
# Mathematics Achievement

# Practice Test 5

*This page intentionally left blank.*

# MA

**4**

| 42 Questions | Time: 36 minutes |
|---|---|

Choose the best answer from the four choices given. Fill in the corresponding circle on your answer document. You may write in the test booklet.

---

SAMPLE QUESTION:                    SAMPLE ANSWER

    What number is 40% of 50?        Ⓐ ● Ⓒ Ⓓ

    (A) 10
    (B) 20
    (C) 30
    (D) 40

    The correct answer is 20, so circle B is darkened.

---

STOP. Do not go on
until told to do so.

**STOP**

1. In the figure, line $p$ is parallel to line $q$.

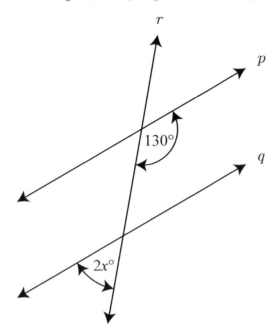

What is the value of $x$?

(A) 25
(B) 50
(C) 65
(D) 130

2. Which expression is equivalent to $(3p - q)(3p + q)$?

(A) $3p^2 - q^2$
(B) $9p^2 - q^2$
(C) $3p^2 - 6pq - q^2$
(D) $9p^2 - 6pq + q^2$

3. For what values of $x$ is it true that $x^4 + x^2 = -1$?

(A) 1 only
(B) $-1$ only
(C) 1 and $-1$
(D) there are no real values of $x$ that make the equation true

4. Chloe recorded the number of students at each lunch table in her school's cafeteria in the chart below.

| Number of Students | Number of lunch tables with that number of students |
|---|---|
| 0 | 4 |
| 1 | 2 |
| 2 | 6 |
| 3 | 7 |
| 4 | $x$ |

Chloe couldn't remember how many tables there were with 4 students, so she put an $x$ in that space. If the correct mode of Chloe's data is 3, which of the following could NOT be the value of $x$?

(A) 3
(B) 5
(C) 6
(D) 8

5. For what value(s) of $x$ does $\dfrac{x+5}{x(x+3)} = 0$?

   (A) $x = -5$ only
   (B) $x = -3$ only
   (C) $x = -5$ and $x = -3$
   (D) $x = -5$ and $x = -3$ and $x = 0$

6. A bowl contains 24 buttons, each of which is either silver or gold. When Bridgette selects two different buttons from the bowl, the probability that both buttons are gold is $\dfrac{7}{24} \times \dfrac{6}{23}$. How many silver buttons were in the bowl before Bridgette selected any buttons?

   (A) 6
   (B) 7
   (C) 17
   (D) 18

7. If $\left(\dfrac{9}{4} - 2.25\right)x - 2 = -2$, which of the following gives all possible values of $x$?

   (A) 0 only
   (B) 0 or 1
   (C) all real numbers
   (D) there are no real values of $x$ that make the equation true

8. The bar chart below shows the number of points earned by Team A and Team B during the six days of a contest.

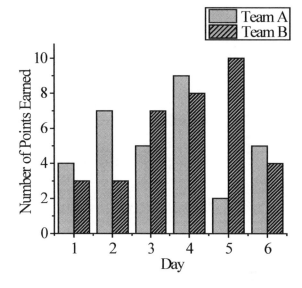

   What is the difference between the median number of points earned per day by Team A and the median number of points earned per day by Team B?

   (A) 2.0
   (B) 1.5
   (C) 1.0
   (D) 0.5

9. Mason has taken one test and two quizzes in his algebra class. Each test counts for two grades in his final average and each quiz counts for one grade. He scored 80 on the test and 90 and 100 on the two quizzes. What must he score on his one remaining test in order for his final average to be 90?

   (A) 100
   (B) 95
   (C) 92
   (D) 90

10. Melanie plays a game in which she gains 1 point 75% of the time and loses 1 point 25% of the time. If Melanie plays the game many times, which of the following best describes her net change in points per play?

    (A) She gains approximately .5 points per play
    (B) She gains approximately .75 points per play
    (C) She loses approximately .25 points per play
    (D) She neither gains nor loses points overall

11. If $3y = y^2$ and $y \neq 3$, what is the value of $y$?

    (A) $-1$
    (B) $0$
    (C) $1$
    (D) it cannot be determined from the information given

12. Caleb, Amelia, Isaac, Riley and Taylor are the participants in a debate. Before the debate, each participant shakes hands with every other participant. How many handshakes take place?

    (A) 5
    (B) 10
    (C) 20
    (D) 25

13. A conical tank is 10 meters high, and the diameter of its open top is 25 meters, as shown in the figure.

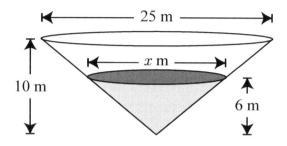

    If the water in the tank reaches a height of 6 meters, what is the value of $x$?

    (A) 21.0
    (B) 16.0
    (C) 15.0
    (D) 2.4

14. $(4.2 \times 10^{-6}) \div (8.4 \times 10^{-3}) =$

    (A) $2 \times 10^{-3}$
    (B) $2 \times 10^{-4}$
    (C) $5 \times 10^{-3}$
    (D) $5 \times 10^{-4}$

15. Which of the following is equal to $\sqrt{9} + \sqrt{25}$?

    (A) $\sqrt{34}$
    (B) $\sqrt{9} + \sqrt{27} - \sqrt{2}$
    (C) $\sqrt{64}$
    (D) $\sqrt{9^2 + 25^2}$

16. Which value is equal to $.0\overline{2}$?

    (A) $\frac{2}{100}$

    (B) $\frac{2}{99}$

    (C) $.1 - .08$

    (D) $1 - .98$

17. Which is the most reasonable unit for measuring the area of a sheet of paper?

    (A) liters
    (B) grams
    (C) square inches
    (D) cubic inches

18. Which expression is equivalent to $3\sqrt{7}$?

    (A) $7\sqrt{3}$
    (B) $\sqrt{21}$
    (C) $\sqrt{63}$
    (D) $\sqrt{147}$

19. If point $(c, 3)$ is on a circle with center $(c, -2)$, what is the length of the diameter of the circle?

    (A) 2 grid units
    (B) 5 grid units
    (C) 10 grid units
    (D) The length of the diameter cannot be determined from the information given

20. Triangle PQR is shown. The length of $\overline{QP}$ is 10 inches. The measure of angle QRP is 25°.

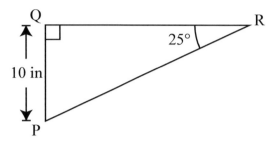

Which expression is equal in value to the length of $\overline{PR}$, in inches?

    (A) $\dfrac{10}{\sin 25°}$

    (B) $10\sin 25°$

    (C) $\dfrac{10}{\tan 25°}$

    (D) $10\tan 25°$

21. An inequality is graphed on the number line shown.

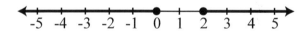

The graph of which inequality is shown?

    (A) $x \geq 2$ or $x \leq 0$
    (B) $x \leq 2$ or $x \geq 0$
    (C) $x \leq 2$ and $x \geq 0$
    (D) $x \geq 2$ and $x \leq 0$

4 **MA**

22. A deck of cards contains 5 red cards, 4 blue cards, and 3 white cards. Martin randomly draws one card from the deck and holds it in his hand. Josie then draws a card from the deck. If Martin's card is blue, what is the probability that Josie's card is also blue?

(A) $\dfrac{4}{12}$

(B) $\dfrac{3}{12}$

(C) $\dfrac{4}{11}$

(D) $\dfrac{3}{11}$

23. Clara was given a list of two-digit numbers and asked to make a stem-and-leaf plot. She made a plot, but she forgot to list any numbers with a tens digit of 4. Her plot is shown.

| Stem | Leaf | | | | | |
|------|------|---|---|---|---|---|
| 2 | 4 | 5 | 5 | 7 | | |
| 3 | 3 | | | | | |
| 4 | | | | | | |
| 5 | 0 | 2 | 4 | 8 | 9 | |
| 6 | 2 | 2 | 3 | 6 | 6 | 7 |
| 7 | 3 | 5 | 6 | 8 | | |

If the correct median of the list Clara was given is 58, how many numbers in the list have a tens digit of 4?

(A) 2

(B) 3

(C) 4

(D) 5

24. Which gives all values of $x$ for which $3 - |2x + 1| < 2$?

(A) $x < -1$

(B) $-1 < x < 0$

(C) $x < -1$ or $x > 0$

(D) all real values of $x$ except $-1$ and $0$

25. What is the solution set for $x^2 = -81$?

(A) 9

(B) $9i$

(C) $\pm 9$

(D) $\pm 9i$

26. The figure shows two concentric circles. The region between them is shaded.

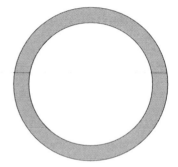

If the radius of the larger circle is 15 feet and the radius of the smaller circle is 12 feet, what is the area of the shaded region?

(A) $9\pi$ square feet

(B) $27\pi$ square feet

(C) $54\pi$ square feet

(D) $81\pi$ square feet

Acadian Academics - Upper Level ISEE Test 5

254

*Go on to the next page.* ➡

27. The graph below shows the number of pets owned by students in Ms. Garcia's class. The numbers on the horizontal axis represent the number of pets owned, and the numbers on the vertical axis represent the number of students who own that number of pets.

Number of Pets Owned by
Students in Ms. Garcia's Class

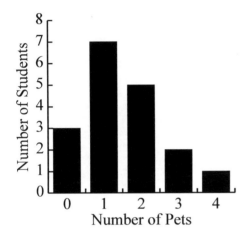

What is the mean number of pets owned?

(A) 1.00
(B) 1.20
(C) 1.25
(D) 1.50

28. Which of the following expressions represents an integer?

(A) $2\sqrt{2}$

(B) $\dfrac{2\sqrt{2}}{\sqrt{2}}$

(C) $\dfrac{2\sqrt{2}}{2}$

(D) $\dfrac{\sqrt{2}}{2}$

29. The grid below shows two vertices of a right triangle.

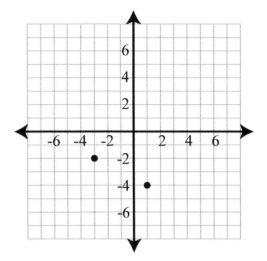

Which of the following could NOT be the third vertex of the triangle?

(A) $(0, -1)$
(B) $(-3, -4)$
(C) $(-1, -5)$
(D) $(1, -2)$

30. The number 615.2 can be written as $x \times 100 + 15 + y \times \left(\frac{1}{10}\right)$, where $x$ and $y$ are integers between 0 and 9, inclusive. What is the product of $x$ and $y$?

(A) 5
(B) 6
(C) 10
(D) 12

31. The graph of a line is shown.

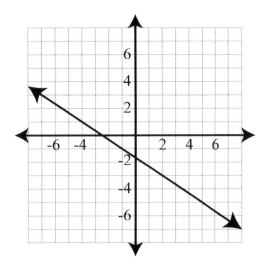

What is the slope of the line?

(A) $-\dfrac{3}{2}$

(B) $-\dfrac{2}{3}$

(C) $\dfrac{2}{3}$

(D) $\dfrac{3}{2}$

32. Which graph represents the solution set of the inequality $-6 + c < 2c < c$?

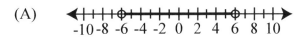

33. Cynthia ate $\dfrac{2}{3}$ of a cake and Alberto ate $\dfrac{1}{4}$ of what remained after Cynthia was finished. What fraction of the whole cake did Alberto eat?

(A) $\dfrac{1}{12}$

(B) $\dfrac{1}{8}$

(C) $\dfrac{1}{6}$

(D) $\dfrac{3}{8}$

34. The price of a stock decreases from $125.00 to $100.00. What is the percent decrease in the price of the stock?

(A) 30.0%

(B) 25.0%

(C) 22.5%

(D) 20.0%

35. A soccer team washes vehicles one weekend to raise money. The team washes twice as many cars as trucks on Saturday and three times as many cars as trucks on Sunday. If the team washes 24 vehicles each day, how many trucks did the team wash over both days?

(A) 8
(B) 14
(C) 22
(D) 34

36. If $s \neq r$, which expression is equivalent to the expression $\frac{r-s}{s-r}$?

(A) $-1$

(B) $0$

(C) $1$

(D) $\frac{r}{s} - \frac{s}{r}$

37. How many irrational numbers are greater than $\sqrt{3}$ but less than $\sqrt{8}$?

(A) 2
(B) 3
(C) 4
(D) more than 4

38. The volume of a sphere is given by the formula $V = \frac{4}{3}\pi r^3$, where $V$ is the volume of the sphere and $r$ is its radius. The figure below shows a sphere inscribed in a cube.

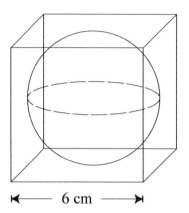

If the length of an edge of the cube is 6 cm, what is the volume of the inscribed sphere?

(A) $4\pi$ cm³
(B) $8\pi$ cm³
(C) $36\pi$ cm³
(D) $288\pi$ cm³

39. If $q$ and $r$ are prime numbers, which of the following is the greatest common factor of $10q^2$, $5qr^2$ and $30qr$?

(A) $30q^2r^2$
(B) $5q$
(C) $30q$
(D) $5q^2r^2$

40. 240 students took a test that is scored on a scale of 0 to 100. Their results are summarized in the box-and-whisker plot below.

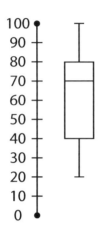

How many students scored between 40 and 70 on the test?

(A) 30
(B) 60
(C) 72
(D) 90

41. Teagan claims that she doesn't like any members of the football team. If some members of the football team are also in the debate club, which of the following, if true, proves Teagan's claim FALSE?

(A) Teagan likes all members of the debate club

(B) Teagan likes at least one member of the debate club

(C) Teagan likes at most one member of the debate club

(D) Teagan doesn't like any members of the debate club

42. The graph shows the altitude of a plane as it begins its descent into an airport.

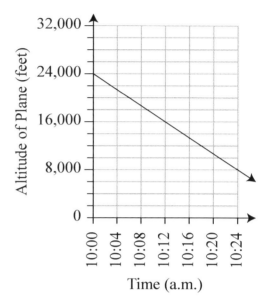

If the plane continues its descent at a constant rate, when will the plane land on the ground?

(A) 10:28 a.m.
(B) 10:32 a.m.
(C) 10:36 a.m.
(D) 10:40 a.m.

Acadian Academics - Upper Level ISEE Test 5

258

STOP. If there is time, you may check your work in this section only.

**STOP**

# Essay Directions

There is an essay topic printed on the next page of this test. Do not turn the page until you are told to begin. Once you are told to begin, you will have 30 minutes to write an essay on the topic provided. You may not write on another topic.

Your writing should be as clear as possible. The quality of your writing is more important than the length of your essay, but your essay should be long enough to develop your ideas and to demonstrate your writing ability.

You may plan your response in the notes section provided on the next page. Any writing you do in the notes section will NOT be counted as part of your essay. Your final draft must be written on the lined portion of your answer sheet. Only what is written on your answer sheet will be considered part of your essay. Remember that you will have only 30 minutes to plan and write your essay, so you should leave enough time to copy your final draft to the answer sheet.

Please use a blue or black pen to write your essay. Do not write outside of the box provided on the answer sheet. You may write in cursive or in print.

Please copy the following topic onto the first few lines of your answer sheet.

# Essay Topic

**Is it important to have daily routines?  Explain why or why not.**

- Do not write on any other topic.
- Write your final draft on the answer sheet, NOT in the space below.
- Write in blue or black pen.

## Notes

_____

_____

_____

_____

_____

_____

_____

_____

_____

_____

_____

_____

_____

_____

_____

# ISEE
Independent School Entrance Exam

# Answer Keys

# Verbal Reasoning Answer Key
# Practice Test 1

| Item | Key | + If Correct | Type | Item | Key | + If Correct | Type |
|------|-----|--------------|------|------|-----|--------------|------|
| 1 | B | | S | 19 | B | | SWR |
| 2 | B | | S | 20 | A | | SWR |
| 3 | A | | S | 21 | B | | SWR |
| 4 | D | | S | 22 | A | | SWR |
| 5 | C | | S | 23 | D | | SWR |
| 6 | A | | S | 24 | C | | SWR |
| 7 | B | | S | 25 | D | | SWR |
| 8 | C | | S | 26 | C | | SWR |
| 9 | D | | S | 27 | B | | SWR |
| 10 | D | | S | 28 | C | | PWR |
| 11 | C | | S | 29 | D | | PWR |
| 12 | A | | S | 30 | A | | PWR |
| 13 | D | | S | 31 | D | | PWR |
| 14 | A | | S | 32 | C | | PWR |
| 15 | B | | S | 33 | D | | PWR |
| 16 | C | | S | 34 | B | | PWR |
| 17 | A | | S | 35 | A | | PWR |
| 18 | C | | SWR | | | | |
| | | | | **Total Correct** | | | |

Type of Item
S = Synonym
SWR = Single Word Response
PWR = Paired Word Response

# Quantitative Reasoning Answer Key
# Practice Test 1

| Item | Key | + If Correct | Type | Item | Key | + If Correct | Type |
|------|-----|--------------|------|------|-----|--------------|------|
| 1 | C | | WP | 17 | B | | WP |
| 2 | D | | WP | 18 | A | | WP |
| 3 | D | | WP | 19 | D | | QC |
| 4 | C | | WP | 20 | A | | QC |
| 5 | A | | WP | 21 | B | | QC |
| 6 | C | | WP | 22 | A | | QC |
| 7 | B | | WP | 23 | C | | QC |
| 8 | B | | WP | 24 | D | | QC |
| 9 | B | | WP | 25 | C | | QC |
| 10 | A | | WP | 26 | A | | QC |
| 11 | A | | WP | 27 | A | | QC |
| 12 | D | | WP | 28 | B | | QC |
| 13 | D | | WP | 29 | C | | QC |
| 14 | A | | WP | 30 | B | | QC |
| 15 | D | | WP | 31 | C | | QC |
| 16 | B | | WP | 32 | D | | QC |
| | | | | **Total Correct** | | | |

Type of Item
WP = Word Problem
QC = Quantitative Comparison

# Reading Comprehension Answer Key
# Practice Test 1

| Item | Key | + If Correct | *Type |
|------|-----|--------------|-------|
| 1 | B | | MI |
| 2 | C | | V |
| 3 | D | | T/S/F |
| 4 | D | | I |
| 5 | B | | SI |
| 6 | A | | T/S/F |
| 7 | B | | I |
| 8 | C | | L/O |
| 9 | C | | V |
| 10 | A | | SI |
| 11 | D | | I |
| 12 | D | | I |
| 13 | A | | L/O |
| 14 | A | | SI |
| 15 | C | | I |
| 16 | B | | MI |
| 17 | B | | SI |
| 18 | B | | SI |
| 19 | C | | I |
| 20 | C | | I |
| 21 | A | | I |
| 22 | D | | SI |
| 23 | B | | SI |
| 24 | C | | SI |
| 25 | C | | MI |
| 26 | A | | L/O |
| 27 | B | | I |
| 28 | A | | T/S/F |
| 29 | D | | SI |
| 30 | D | | SI |
| Total Correct | | | |

| | | *Key to Type of Item |
|---|---|---|
| MI | = | Main Idea |
| SI | = | Supporting Idea |
| I | = | Inference |
| V | = | Vocabulary |
| L/O | = | Logic/Organization |
| T/S/F | = | Tone/Style/Figurative Language |

# Mathematics Achievement Answer Key
# Practice Test 1

| Item | Key | + If Correct | Item | Key | + If Correct |
|------|-----|--------------|------|-----|--------------|
| 1 | C | | 22 | C | |
| 2 | A | | 23 | D | |
| 3 | A | | 24 | C | |
| 4 | D | | 25 | C | |
| 5 | A | | 26 | B | |
| 6 | D | | 27 | A | |
| 7 | B | | 28 | A | |
| 8 | C | | 29 | B | |
| 9 | B | | 30 | C | |
| 10 | C | | 31 | D | |
| 11 | B | | 32 | C | |
| 12 | A | | 33 | B | |
| 13 | B | | 34 | C | |
| 14 | B | | 35 | D | |
| 15 | C | | 36 | B | |
| 16 | B | | 37 | D | |
| 17 | D | | 38 | A | |
| 18 | A | | 39 | D | |
| 19 | A | | 40 | A | |
| 20 | B | | 41 | D | |
| 21 | A | | 42 | D | |
| | | | **Total Correct** | | |

# Verbal Reasoning Answer Key
# Practice Test 2

| Item | Key | + If Correct | Type | Item | Key | + If Correct | Type |
|------|-----|--------------|------|------|-----|--------------|------|
| 1 | D | | S | 19 | D | | SWR |
| 2 | C | | S | 20 | B | | SWR |
| 3 | A | | S | 21 | B | | SWR |
| 4 | A | | S | 22 | C | | SWR |
| 5 | C | | S | 23 | B | | SWR |
| 6 | B | | S | 24 | B | | SWR |
| 7 | A | | S | 25 | C | | SWR |
| 8 | A | | S | 26 | B | | SWR |
| 9 | D | | S | 27 | C | | SWR |
| 10 | B | | S | 28 | A | | PWR |
| 11 | B | | S | 29 | A | | PWR |
| 12 | C | | S | 30 | D | | PWR |
| 13 | C | | S | 31 | D | | PWR |
| 14 | B | | S | 32 | A | | PWR |
| 15 | D | | S | 33 | D | | PWR |
| 16 | B | | S | 34 | A | | PWR |
| 17 | C | | S | 35 | C | | PWR |
| 18 | A | | SWR | | | | |
| | | | | **Total Correct** | | | |

Type of Item
S = Synonym
SWR = Single Word Response
PWR = Paired Word Response

# Quantitative Reasoning Answer Key
# Practice Test 2

| Item | Key | + If Correct | Type | Item | Key | + If Correct | Type |
|------|-----|--------------|------|------|-----|--------------|------|
| 1 | A | | WP | 17 | C | | WP |
| 2 | D | | WP | 18 | C | | WP |
| 3 | B | | WP | 19 | D | | QC |
| 4 | D | | WP | 20 | D | | QC |
| 5 | C | | WP | 21 | C | | QC |
| 6 | D | | WP | 22 | B | | QC |
| 7 | A | | WP | 23 | C | | QC |
| 8 | D | | WP | 24 | C | | QC |
| 9 | D | | WP | 25 | B | | QC |
| 10 | B | | WP | 26 | D | | QC |
| 11 | C | | WP | 27 | D | | QC |
| 12 | C | | WP | 28 | A | | QC |
| 13 | A | | WP | 29 | C | | QC |
| 14 | B | | WP | 30 | C | | QC |
| 15 | A | | WP | 31 | B | | QC |
| 16 | B | | WP | 32 | B | | QC |
| | | | | **Total Correct** | | | |

Type of Item
WP = Word Problem
QC = Quantitative Comparison

# Reading Comprehension Answer Key
## Practice Test 2

| Item | Key | + If Correct | *Type |
|------|-----|-------------|-------|
| 1 | B | | SI |
| 2 | C | | I |
| 3 | D | | SI |
| 4 | A | | I |
| 5 | D | | SI |
| 6 | C | | V |
| 7 | D | | I |
| 8 | B | | I |
| 9 | A | | I |
| 10 | B | | V |
| 11 | C | | SI |
| 12 | A | | SI |
| 13 | B | | SI |
| 14 | C | | MI |
| 15 | D | | T/S/F |
| 16 | B | | V |
| 17 | A | | T/S/F |
| 18 | D | | I |
| 19 | C | | T/S/F |
| 20 | A | | L/O |
| 21 | D | | SI |
| 22 | A | | I |
| 23 | C | | V |
| 24 | B | | MI |
| 25 | C | | T/S/F |
| 26 | A | | T/S/F |
| 27 | B | | V |
| 28 | D | | I |
| 29 | D | | SI |
| 30 | B | | I |
| Total Correct | | | |

*Key to Type of Item

| | | |
|------|---|---|
| MI | = | Main Idea |
| SI | = | Supporting Idea |
| I | = | Inference |
| V | = | Vocabulary |
| L/O | = | Logic/Organization |
| T/S/F | = | Tone/Style/Figurative Language |

# Mathematics Achievement Answer Key
## Practice Test 2

| Item | Key | + If Correct | Item | Key | + If Correct |
|------|-----|--------------|------|-----|--------------|
| 1 | D | | 22 | A | |
| 2 | B | | 23 | C | |
| 3 | D | | 24 | B | |
| 4 | C | | 25 | B | |
| 5 | B | | 26 | A | |
| 6 | D | | 27 | B | |
| 7 | A | | 28 | B | |
| 8 | C | | 29 | A | |
| 9 | A | | 30 | A | |
| 10 | A | | 31 | D | |
| 11 | C | | 32 | A | |
| 12 | B | | 33 | D | |
| 13 | C | | 34 | A | |
| 14 | C | | 35 | A | |
| 15 | D | | 36 | C | |
| 16 | C | | 37 | B | |
| 17 | D | | 38 | A | |
| 18 | B | | 39 | D | |
| 19 | B | | 40 | D | |
| 20 | C | | 41 | D | |
| 21 | C | | 42 | D | |
| | | | **Total Correct** | | |

# Verbal Reasoning Answer Key
## Practice Test 3

| Item | Key | + If Correct | Type | Item | Key | + If Correct | Type |
|------|-----|--------------|------|------|-----|--------------|------|
| 1 | D | | S | 19 | B | | SWR |
| 2 | A | | S | 20 | A | | SWR |
| 3 | D | | S | 21 | D | | SWR |
| 4 | C | | S | 22 | D | | SWR |
| 5 | C | | S | 23 | D | | SWR |
| 6 | A | | S | 24 | B | | SWR |
| 7 | B | | S | 25 | A | | SWR |
| 8 | A | | S | 26 | C | | SWR |
| 9 | A | | S | 27 | C | | SWR |
| 10 | C | | S | 28 | B | | PWR |
| 11 | D | | S | 29 | A | | PWR |
| 12 | B | | S | 30 | B | | PWR |
| 13 | B | | S | 31 | D | | PWR |
| 14 | C | | S | 32 | C | | PWR |
| 15 | A | | S | 33 | D | | PWR |
| 16 | B | | S | 34 | A | | PWR |
| 17 | D | | S | 35 | B | | PWR |
| 18 | C | | SWR | **Total Correct** | | | |

> Type of Item
> S = Synonym
> SWR = Single Word Response
> PWR = Paired Word Response

# Quantitative Reasoning Answer Key
# Practice Test 3

| Item | Key | + If Correct | Type | Item | Key | + If Correct | Type |
|------|-----|--------------|------|------|-----|--------------|------|
| 1 | B | | WP | 17 | D | | WP |
| 2 | C | | WP | 18 | C | | WP |
| 3 | C | | WP | 19 | B | | QC |
| 4 | C | | WP | 20 | C | | QC |
| 5 | A | | WP | 21 | B | | QC |
| 6 | B | | WP | 22 | A | | QC |
| 7 | A | | WP | 23 | A | | QC |
| 8 | C | | WP | 24 | B | | QC |
| 9 | A | | WP | 25 | A | | QC |
| 10 | D | | WP | 26 | D | | QC |
| 11 | D | | WP | 27 | D | | QC |
| 12 | B | | WP | 28 | A | | QC |
| 13 | B | | WP | 29 | A | | QC |
| 14 | D | | WP | 30 | C | | QC |
| 15 | C | | WP | 31 | D | | QC |
| 16 | B | | WP | 32 | B | | QC |
| | | | | **Total Correct** | | | |

| Type of Item |
|---|
| WP = Word Problem |
| QC = Quantitative Comparison |

# Reading Comprehension Answer Key
# Practice Test 3

| Item | Key | + If Correct | *Type |
|------|-----|--------------|-------|
| 1 | C | | MI |
| 2 | A | | SI |
| 3 | A | | I |
| 4 | A | | L/O |
| 5 | B | | I |
| 6 | D | | SI |
| 7 | C | | SI |
| 8 | B | | SI |
| 9 | C | | MI |
| 10 | C | | SI |
| 11 | A | | L/O |
| 12 | B | | V |
| 13 | B | | V |
| 14 | A | | I |
| 15 | D | | T/S/F |
| 16 | D | | SI |
| 17 | C | | SI |
| 18 | C | | MI |
| 19 | B | | MI |
| 20 | D | | SI |
| 21 | D | | V |
| 22 | A | | I |
| 23 | A | | L/O |
| 24 | C | | SI |
| 25 | C | | MI |
| 26 | A | | L/O |
| 27 | D | | T/S/F |
| 28 | B | | I |
| 29 | B | | SI |
| 30 | D | | T/S/F |
| Total Correct | | | |

### *Key to Type of Item

| | | |
|------|---|---------------------|
| MI | = | Main Idea |
| SI | = | Supporting Idea |
| I | = | Inference |
| V | = | Vocabulary |
| L/O | = | Logic/Organization |
| T/S/F | = | Tone/Style/Figurative Language |

# Mathematics Achievement Answer Key
# Practice Test 3

| Item | Key | + If Correct | Item | Key | + If Correct |
|------|-----|--------------|------|-----|--------------|
| 1 | D | | 22 | C | |
| 2 | C | | 23 | B | |
| 3 | B | | 24 | D | |
| 4 | B | | 25 | B | |
| 5 | C | | 26 | C | |
| 6 | A | | 27 | A | |
| 7 | D | | 28 | A | |
| 8 | D | | 29 | C | |
| 9 | D | | 30 | A | |
| 10 | A | | 31 | D | |
| 11 | C | | 32 | B | |
| 12 | B | | 33 | C | |
| 13 | C | | 34 | A | |
| 14 | B | | 35 | B | |
| 15 | C | | 36 | D | |
| 16 | A | | 37 | D | |
| 17 | A | | 38 | A | |
| 18 | B | | 39 | B | |
| 19 | A | | 40 | C | |
| 20 | D | | 41 | A | |
| 21 | C | | 42 | D | |
| | | | **Total Correct** | | |

# Verbal Reasoning Answer Key
# Practice Test 4

| Item | Key | + If Correct | Type | Item | Key | + If Correct | Type |
|------|-----|--------------|------|------|-----|--------------|------|
| 1 | A | | S | 19 | A | | SWR |
| 2 | C | | S | 20 | A | | SWR |
| 3 | A | | S | 21 | C | | SWR |
| 4 | B | | S | 22 | A | | SWR |
| 5 | C | | S | 23 | B | | SWR |
| 6 | B | | S | 24 | C | | SWR |
| 7 | D | | S | 25 | D | | SWR |
| 8 | D | | S | 26 | C | | SWR |
| 9 | B | | S | 27 | C | | SWR |
| 10 | A | | S | 28 | D | | PWR |
| 11 | D | | S | 29 | B | | PWR |
| 12 | D | | S | 30 | C | | PWR |
| 13 | B | | S | 31 | B | | PWR |
| 14 | D | | S | 32 | D | | PWR |
| 15 | A | | S | 33 | B | | PWR |
| 16 | C | | S | 34 | A | | PWR |
| 17 | C | | S | 35 | D | | PWR |
| 18 | B | | SWR | | | | |
| | | | | **Total Correct** | | | |

| Type of Item |
|---|
| S = Synonym |
| SWR = Single Word Response |
| PWR = Paired Word Response |

# Quantitative Reasoning Answer Key
# Practice Test 4

| Item | Key | + If Correct | Type | Item | Key | + If Correct | Type |
|------|-----|--------------|------|------|-----|--------------|------|
| 1 | C | | WP | 17 | D | | WP |
| 2 | D | | WP | 18 | D | | WP |
| 3 | A | | WP | 19 | A | | QC |
| 4 | D | | WP | 20 | B | | QC |
| 5 | B | | WP | 21 | C | | QC |
| 6 | C | | WP | 22 | D | | QC |
| 7 | A | | WP | 23 | A | | QC |
| 8 | C | | WP | 24 | D | | QC |
| 9 | B | | WP | 25 | C | | QC |
| 10 | A | | WP | 26 | D | | QC |
| 11 | B | | WP | 27 | A | | QC |
| 12 | C | | WP | 28 | D | | QC |
| 13 | C | | WP | 29 | C | | QC |
| 14 | B | | WP | 30 | B | | QC |
| 15 | D | | WP | 31 | A | | QC |
| 16 | A | | WP | 32 | C | | QC |
| | | | | **Total Correct** | | | |

Type of Item
WP = Word Problem
QC = Quantitative Comparison

# Reading Comprehension Answer Key
# Practice Test 4

| Item | Key | + If Correct | *Type |
|------|-----|--------------|-------|
| 1 | C | | MI |
| 2 | D | | SI |
| 3 | B | | I |
| 4 | B | | L/O |
| 5 | A | | SI |
| 6 | D | | SI |
| 7 | A | | L/O |
| 8 | C | | SI |
| 9 | D | | SI |
| 10 | C | | I |
| 11 | A | | I |
| 12 | D | | V |
| 13 | C | | SI |
| 14 | A | | I |
| 15 | B | | MI |
| 16 | A | | I |
| 17 | B | | I |
| 18 | C | | V |
| 19 | D | | MI |
| 20 | A | | I |
| 21 | C | | SI |
| 22 | B | | SI |
| 23 | C | | L/O |
| 24 | D | | I |
| 25 | B | | I |
| 26 | A | | SI |
| 27 | D | | MI |
| 28 | C | | SI |
| 29 | D | | L/O |
| 30 | A | | SI |
| Total Correct | | | |

*Key to Type of Item

| | | |
|------|---|---|
| MI | = | Main Idea |
| SI | = | Supporting Idea |
| I | = | Inference |
| V | = | Vocabulary |
| L/O | = | Logic/Organization |
| T/S/F | = | Tone/Style/Figurative Language |

# Mathematics Achievement Answer Key
# Practice Test 4

| Item | Key | + If Correct | Item | Key | + If Correct |
|------|-----|--------------|------|-----|--------------|
| 1 | D | | 22 | B | |
| 2 | B | | 23 | C | |
| 3 | A | | 24 | A | |
| 4 | A | | 25 | D | |
| 5 | D | | 26 | B | |
| 6 | A | | 27 | B | |
| 7 | B | | 28 | B | |
| 8 | C | | 29 | D | |
| 9 | A | | 30 | C | |
| 10 | C | | 31 | B | |
| 11 | D | | 32 | D | |
| 12 | C | | 33 | C | |
| 13 | D | | 34 | B | |
| 14 | D | | 35 | C | |
| 15 | A | | 36 | B | |
| 16 | A | | 37 | C | |
| 17 | C | | 38 | B | |
| 18 | D | | 39 | B | |
| 19 | D | | 40 | C | |
| 20 | A | | 41 | A | |
| 21 | D | | 42 | D | |
| | | | **Total Correct** | | |

# Verbal Reasoning Answer Key
# Practice Test 5

| Item | Key | + If Correct | Type | Item | Key | + If Correct | Type |
|------|-----|-------------|------|------|-----|-------------|------|
| 1 | B | | S | 19 | B | | SWR |
| 2 | A | | S | 20 | A | | SWR |
| 3 | C | | S | 21 | A | | SWR |
| 4 | D | | S | 22 | D | | SWR |
| 5 | B | | S | 23 | D | | SWR |
| 6 | D | | S | 24 | B | | SWR |
| 7 | A | | S | 25 | D | | SWR |
| 8 | C | | S | 26 | C | | SWR |
| 9 | D | | S | 27 | C | | SWR |
| 10 | B | | S | 28 | C | | PWR |
| 11 | A | | S | 29 | C | | PWR |
| 12 | A | | S | 30 | A | | PWR |
| 13 | C | | S | 31 | A | | PWR |
| 14 | B | | S | 32 | B | | PWR |
| 15 | D | | S | 33 | D | | PWR |
| 16 | B | | S | 34 | B | | PWR |
| 17 | D | | S | 35 | A | | PWR |
| 18 | D | | SWR | | | | |
| | | | | **Total Correct** | | | |

> Type of Item
> S = Synonym
> SWR = Single Word Response
> PWR = Paired Word Response

# Quantitative Reasoning Answer Key
# Practice Test 5

| Item | Key | + If Correct | Type | Item | Key | + If Correct | Type |
|------|-----|------|------|------|-----|------|------|
| 1 | B | | WP | 17 | D | | WP |
| 2 | C | | WP | 18 | B | | WP |
| 3 | A | | WP | 19 | C | | QC |
| 4 | C | | WP | 20 | B | | QC |
| 5 | D | | WP | 21 | D | | QC |
| 6 | B | | WP | 22 | D | | QC |
| 7 | A | | WP | 23 | A | | QC |
| 8 | D | | WP | 24 | B | | QC |
| 9 | D | | WP | 25 | B | | QC |
| 10 | B | | WP | 26 | A | | QC |
| 11 | C | | WP | 27 | C | | QC |
| 12 | D | | WP | 28 | D | | QC |
| 13 | A | | WP | 29 | C | | QC |
| 14 | A | | WP | 30 | A | | QC |
| 15 | A | | WP | 31 | B | | QC |
| 16 | C | | WP | 32 | D | | QC |
| | | | | **Total Correct** | | | |

| Type of Item |
|---|
| WP = Word Problem |
| QC = Quantitative Comparison |

# Reading Comprehension Answer Key
# Practice Test 5

| Item | Key | + If Correct | *Type |
|------|-----|--------------|-------|
| 1 | C | | MI |
| 2 | A | | L/O |
| 3 | D | | V |
| 4 | C | | I |
| 5 | D | | SI |
| 6 | B | | SI |
| 7 | B | | V |
| 8 | A | | L/O |
| 9 | C | | MI |
| 10 | D | | SI |
| 11 | B | | SI |
| 12 | B | | SI |
| 13 | A | | MI |
| 14 | A | | V |
| 15 | B | | I |
| 16 | D | | SI |
| 17 | B | | I |
| 18 | C | | T/S/F |
| 19 | D | | SI |
| 20 | D | | SI |
| 21 | C | | I |
| 22 | A | | L/O |
| 23 | C | | MI |
| 24 | A | | T/S/F |
| 25 | B | | L/O |
| 26 | D | | T/S/F |
| 27 | A | | MI |
| 28 | B | | SI |
| 29 | A | | I |
| 30 | C | | SI |
| Total Correct | | | |

*Key to Type of Item

| | | |
|------|---|-------------------------|
| MI | = | Main Idea |
| SI | = | Supporting Idea |
| I | = | Inference |
| V | = | Vocabulary |
| L/O | = | Logic/Organization |
| T/S/F | = | Tone/Style/Figurative Language |

# Mathematics Achievement Answer Key
## Practice Test 5

| Item | Key | + If Correct | Item | Key | + If Correct |
|------|-----|-------------|------|-----|-------------|
| 1 | A | | 22 | D | |
| 2 | B | | 23 | B | |
| 3 | D | | 24 | C | |
| 4 | D | | 25 | D | |
| 5 | A | | 26 | D | |
| 6 | C | | 27 | D | |
| 7 | C | | 28 | B | |
| 8 | D | | 29 | C | |
| 9 | B | | 30 | D | |
| 10 | A | | 31 | B | |
| 11 | B | | 32 | C | |
| 12 | B | | 33 | A | |
| 13 | C | | 34 | D | |
| 14 | D | | 35 | B | |
| 15 | C | | 36 | A | |
| 16 | B | | 37 | D | |
| 17 | C | | 38 | C | |
| 18 | C | | 39 | B | |
| 19 | C | | 40 | B | |
| 20 | A | | 41 | A | |
| 21 | A | | 42 | C | |
| | | | **Total Correct** | | |

# Scoring Instructions

Your practice test score consists of three parts for each of the four multiple-choice sections.

- Your *raw score* is the number of questions you answered correctly.

- Your *scaled score* is a number between 760 and 940 that can be used to compare your performance to that of students who took similar tests.

- Your *stanine score* gives a range for your percentile rank, which is the percentage of students who scored lower on the test than you did. The correspondence between stanine scores and percentile ranks is as follows:

| Stanine | 1 | 2 | 3 | 4 | 5 | 6 | 7 | 8 | 9 |
|---|---|---|---|---|---|---|---|---|---|
| Percentile Range | 1-3% | 4-10% | 11-22% | 23-39% | 40-59% | 60-76% | 77-88% | 89-95% | 96-99% |

## Scoring Your Test

1. Compare your answers to the answers given on the answer key. For each correct answer, mark a + sign in the appropriate row on the answer key. Leave the space blank if you didn't answer the question or you answered the question incorrectly.
2. Count the number of correct answers. Enter the result in the row labeled "Total Correct." This number is your raw score.
3. Locate your raw score in the "raw score" column of the appropriate table on pages 283-286. The corresponding number in the "scaled score" column is your scaled score. The corresponding number in the "stanine" column is your stanine score.

# Verbal Reasoning Conversion Table

| Raw Score | Scaled Score | Stanine | Raw Score | Scaled Score | Stanine |
|-----------|--------------|---------|-----------|--------------|---------|
| 35 | 925 | 9 | 17 | 873 | 4 |
| 34 | 922 | 9 | 16 | 870 | 4 |
| 33 | 919 | 9 | 15 | 867 | 4 |
| 32 | 917 | 9 | 14 | 864 | 3 |
| 31 | 914 | 8 | 13 | 861 | 3 |
| 30 | 911 | 8 | 12 | 859 | 3 |
| 29 | 908 | 8 | 11 | 856 | 3 |
| 28 | 905 | 8 | 10 | 853 | 2 |
| 27 | 902 | 7 | 9 | 850 | 2 |
| 26 | 899 | 7 | 8 | 847 | 2 |
| 25 | 896 | 7 | 7 | 844 | 1 |
| 24 | 893 | 6 | 6 | 841 | 1 |
| 23 | 890 | 6 | 5 | 838 | 1 |
| 22 | 888 | 6 | 4 | 835 | 1 |
| 21 | 885 | 5 | 3 | 832 | 1 |
| 20 | 882 | 5 | 2 | 829 | 1 |
| 19 | 879 | 5 | 1 | 826 | 1 |
| 18 | 876 | 5 | 0 | 823 | 1 |

# Quantitative Reasoning Conversion Table

| Raw Score | Scaled Score | Stanine | Raw Score | Scaled Score | Stanine |
|---|---|---|---|---|---|
| 32 | 930 | 9 | 15 | 873 | 4 |
| 31 | 927 | 9 | 14 | 869 | 4 |
| 30 | 923 | 9 | 13 | 866 | 4 |
| 29 | 920 | 9 | 12 | 862 | 3 |
| 28 | 916 | 8 | 11 | 859 | 3 |
| 27 | 913 | 8 | 10 | 855 | 3 |
| 26 | 909 | 8 | 9 | 852 | 2 |
| 25 | 906 | 8 | 8 | 848 | 2 |
| 24 | 903 | 7 | 7 | 845 | 2 |
| 23 | 899 | 7 | 6 | 842 | 1 |
| 22 | 896 | 7 | 5 | 838 | 1 |
| 21 | 893 | 6 | 4 | 835 | 1 |
| 20 | 889 | 6 | 3 | 832 | 1 |
| 19 | 886 | 6 | 2 | 829 | 1 |
| 18 | 883 | 5 | 1 | 825 | 1 |
| 17 | 879 | 5 | 0 | 822 | 1 |
| 16 | 876 | 5 | | | |

# Reading Comprehension Conversion Table

| Raw Score | Scaled Score | Stanine | Raw Score | Scaled Score | Stanine |
|:---:|:---:|:---:|:---:|:---:|:---:|
| 30 | 924 | 9 | 14 | 864 | 4 |
| 29 | 920 | 9 | 13 | 860 | 3 |
| 28 | 917 | 8 | 12 | 856 | 3 |
| 27 | 913 | 8 | 11 | 853 | 3 |
| 26 | 909 | 7 | 10 | 849 | 2 |
| 25 | 905 | 7 | 9 | 845 | 2 |
| 24 | 902 | 7 | 8 | 842 | 2 |
| 23 | 898 | 6 | 7 | 838 | 1 |
| 22 | 894 | 6 | 6 | 834 | 1 |
| 21 | 890 | 6 | 5 | 831 | 1 |
| 20 | 887 | 5 | 4 | 827 | 1 |
| 19 | 883 | 5 | 3 | 823 | 1 |
| 18 | 879 | 5 | 2 | 819 | 1 |
| 17 | 875 | 5 | 1 | 816 | 1 |
| 16 | 872 | 4 | 0 | 812 | 1 |
| 15 | 868 | 4 | | | |

# Mathematics Achievement Conversion Table

| Raw Score | Scaled Score | Stanine | Raw Score | Scaled Score | Stanine |
|---|---|---|---|---|---|
| 42 | 935 | 9 | 20 | 876 | 5 |
| 41 | 932 | 9 | 19 | 873 | 4 |
| 40 | 930 | 9 | 18 | 870 | 4 |
| 39 | 927 | 9 | 17 | 868 | 4 |
| 38 | 924 | 9 | 16 | 865 | 3 |
| 37 | 922 | 8 | 15 | 862 | 3 |
| 36 | 919 | 8 | 14 | 860 | 3 |
| 35 | 916 | 8 | 13 | 857 | 2 |
| 34 | 913 | 8 | 12 | 854 | 2 |
| 33 | 911 | 8 | 11 | 852 | 2 |
| 32 | 908 | 7 | 10 | 849 | 2 |
| 31 | 905 | 7 | 9 | 846 | 1 |
| 30 | 903 | 7 | 8 | 843 | 1 |
| 29 | 900 | 7 | 7 | 841 | 1 |
| 28 | 897 | 7 | 6 | 838 | 1 |
| 27 | 895 | 6 | 5 | 835 | 1 |
| 26 | 892 | 6 | 4 | 833 | 1 |
| 25 | 889 | 6 | 3 | 830 | 1 |
| 24 | 887 | 6 | 2 | 827 | 1 |
| 23 | 884 | 5 | 1 | 824 | 1 |
| 22 | 881 | 5 | 0 | 822 | 1 |
| 21 | 878 | 5 | | | |

Printed in Poland
by Amazon Fulfillment
Poland Sp. z o.o., Wrocław